CHANGING RESIDENCE

THE GEOGRAPHIC MOBILITY
OF ELDERLY CANADIANS

by

Herbert C. Northcott

University of Alberta

Butterworths
Toronto and Vancouver

Changing Residence: The Geographic Mobility of Elderly Canadians
© 1988 Butterworths, A division of Reed Inc.

Printed and bound in Canada

The Butterworth Group of Companies
Canada
Butterworths, Toronto and Vancouver
United Kingdom
Butterworth & Co. (Publishers) Ltd., London and Edinburgh
Australia
Butterworth Pty Ltd., Sydney, Melbourne, Brisbane, Adelaide and Perth
New Zealand
Butterworths (New Zealand) Ltd., Wellington and Auckland
Singapore
Butterworth & Co. (Asia) Pte., Singapore
United States
Butterworth Legal Publishers, Boston, Seattle, Austin and St. Paul
D&S Publishers, Clearwater

Canadian Cataloguing in Publication Data
Northcott, Herbert C., 1947–
    Changing residence: the geographic mobility of
elderly Canadians

(Perspectives on individual and population aging)
Bibliography: p.
Includes index.
ISBN 0-409-81147-5

1. Residential mobility – Canada.   2. Migration,
Internal – Canada.   3. Aged – Canada.   I. Title.
II. Series.

HB1989.N67 1988   304.8'0971   C87-094976-4

Sponsoring Editor: Janet Turner
Executive Editor (P. & A.): Lebby Hines
Managing Editor: Linda Kee
Supervisory Editor: Marie Graham
Editor: Robert Goodfellow
Cover Design: Patrick Ng
Production: Jill Thomson

BUTTERWORTHS PERSPECTIVES ON INDIVIDUAL AND POPULATION AGING SERIES

The initiation of this Series represents an exciting and significant development for gerontology in Canada. Since the production of Canadian-based knowledge about individual and population aging is expanding rapidly, students, scholars and practitioners are seeking comprehensive yet succinct summaries of the literature on specific topics. Recognizing the common need of this diverse community of gerontologists, Janet Turner, Sponsoring Editor at Butterworths, conceived the idea of a series of specialized monographs that could be used in gerontology courses to complement existing texts and, at the same time, to serve as a valuable reference for those initiating research, developing policies, or providing services to elderly Canadians.

Each monograph includes a state-of-the-art review and analysis of the Canadian-based scientific and professional knowledge on the topic. Where appropriate for comparative purposes, information from other countries is introduced. In addition, some important policy and program implications of the current knowledge base are discussed, and unanswered policy and research questions are raised to stimulate further work in the area. The monographs have been written for a wide audience: undergraduate students in a variety of gerontology courses; graduate students and research personnel who need a summary and analysis of the Canadian literature prior to initiating research projects; practitioners who are involved in the daily planning and delivery of services to aging adults; and policy-makers who require current and reliable information in order to design, implement and evaluate policies and legislation for an aging population.

The decision to publish a monograph on a specific topic has been based in part on the relevance of the topic for the academic and professional community, as well as on the extent of information available at the time an author is signed to a contract. Thus, not all the conceivable topics are included in the early stages of the Series and some topics are published earlier rather than later. Because gerontology in Canada is attracting large numbers of highly qualified graduate students as well as increasingly active research personnel in academic, public and private settings, new areas of concentrated research will evolve. Hence, additional monographs that review and analyze work in these areas will be needed to reflect the evolution of knowledge on specialized topics pertaining to individual or population aging in Canada.

Before introducing the seventh monograph in the Series, I would like, on behalf of the Series' authors and the gerontology community, to acknowledge the following members of the Butterworths "team" and their respective staffs for their unique and sincere contribution to gerontology in Canada: Geoffrey Burn, President, for his continuing support of the project despite difficult times in the Canadian publishing industry; Janet Turner, Sponsoring Editor, for her vision, endurance and high academic standards; Linda Kee, Managing Editor, for her co-ordination of the production, especially her constant reminders to authors (and the Series Editor) that the hands of the clock continue to move in spite of our perceptions that manuscript deadlines were still months or years away; Jim Shepherd, Production Manager, for nimbly vaulting many a technical obstacle; and Gloria Vitale, Academic Sales Manager, for her support and promotion of the Series. For each of you, we hope the knowledge provided in this Series will have personal value — but not until well into the next century!

Barry D. McPherson
Series Editor

FOREWORD

With the onset of population aging, "gray" areas of residential concentration within a country or region became increasingly visible as long-term residents aged "in place." As a consequence, a myth has evolved that the elderly are geographically stable and generally immobile, at least until forced to move into an institution. Yet, as recent evidence in a number of countries has shown, with increased health and economic status, and with higher rates of mobility earlier in the life cycle, there is considerable residential movement among older adults, especially immediately following retirement. These voluntary moves may be local within a municipal boundary, or they may involve intraprovincial, interprovincial or international migration, although for Canadians much of the international migration is seasonal rather than permanent.

An understanding of the consequences of geographic mobility for the sending and receiving areas, and of the degree of net migration in a given area, is essential for policy planning and program delivery. Hence, the study of the patterns, determinants and consequences of the geographic mobility of older Canadians has become of increasing interest to geographers, demographers, planners, economists, gerontologists, politicians, and health care and social service personnel, as well as for private entrepreneurs in the communities which the elderly enter or leave. To illustrate, a single demographic profile of British Columbia, Saskatchewan and the Atlantic Provinces would identify these areas as "gray" regions. However, each area is unique, and the real economic, social and political consequences of this situation can only be fully understood when we learn, for example, that British Columbia is "graying" because there is a large in-migration of older Canadians. In contrast, Saskatchewan and the Atlantic Provinces are "graying" because there is a large out-migration of younger Canadians, and a tendency for older adults in these regions to "age in place." Similar patterns can occur within specific communities or neighbourhoods throughout Canada.

This monograph focuses on the patterns of migration by older adults, on the consequences of this movement for both the individual and the communities which gain or lose elderly residents, on the implications of Canadian policies for elderly migration, and on the impact of later life migration for Canadian policies. Professor Northcott critically reviews the current literature, dissects existing census data pertaining to migration, and presents a number of analyses that were completed specifically for this monograph. Moreover, migration patterns in Canada are compared to those for Australia, France, Great Britain and the United States. Throughout, the author employs a socio-demographic approach to mobility. This approach involves an analysis of the *objective* characteristics of various population subgroups (for example, defined by age, gender, socio-economic status, education, marital status and mother tongue) and of various sending and receiving locations (that is, communities, provinces, regions); and, an analysis of the *subjective* characteristics of individuals who move or stay in place (that is, attitudes, values, beliefs and perceptions).

In Chapters 1 and 2 we are introduced to the concepts, typologies, models and theories that are essential for studying the geographic mobility of older Canadians, particularly with respect to four important dimensions: the permanence, distance, motivation for and type of move. Employing census data, as well as address changes reported by recipients of Old Age Security cheques, Professor Northcott includes in Chapters 3 and 4 a description and discussion of the types, rates and patterns of mobility by older Canadians. In addition, cohort comparisons are introduced to illustrate changing patterns by age within the older cohort (sixty-five years of age and older), both for the 1981 Census and for earlier cohorts of elderly Canadians. It is clearly shown that the elderly move or stay in place for a variety of reasons. In Chapter 5 Canadian mobility patterns are compared with those in four other countries. The final two chapters present a discussion of the two-way interaction between geographic mobility and policies pertaining to retirement, housing, Old Age Security, health care, and immigration. In addition, like other monographs in the Series, the final chapters introduce important research questions that need to be addressed.

In summary, the geographic mobility of older Canadians represents a new area of inquiry and analysis. Yet, as this monograph shows, we already have some understanding of the topic. One major element of this understanding is that the current cohort of elderly Canadians is more mobile than previous cohorts. However, older Canadians are generally less mobile than Americans, and most moves are temporary rather than permanent, and local rather than long distance. But, the patterns and consequences are expected to change in the future as younger cohorts move more frequently throughout their lifecourse. Moreover, the motivations for moving in the later years are becoming more diverse. They include: a voluntary change in life-style (for example, a seasonal move to a warmer climate, a move to the suburbs or a rural location); a desire to return to one's "roots" or to live close to relatives; an amenity move from a house to an apartment or condominium; or a move into an institutional setting.

With the publication of this monograph, we now have a baseline of information and an agenda for further policy analysis and research. Clearly, policy-makers and practitioners will be sensitized to the increasing importance of geographic mobility as a significant factor in planning policies and programs for older Canadians. At the same time, this monograph should stimulate considerable multi-disciplinary research on the geographic mobility patterns of future cohorts of older Canadians.

Barry D. McPherson, Ph.D
Series Editor
Waterloo, Ontario, Canada
October 1987

PREFACE

While geographic mobility per se has long been of great interest to demographers, economists, social planners, and others, the geographic mobility of older persons has been neglected until very recently. In the past, the elderly constituted a relatively small proportion of the population and were less likely than younger age groups to change their places of residence. Further, the older population is less likely to move for economic reasons (for example, jobs) and more likely to move for non-economic reasons (for example, health, recreation) than is the non-elderly population. Therefore, it was the economically motivated geographic mobility of the non-elderly that dominated the attention of those who have studied the patterns, determinants, and consequences of residential change. Recently, however, the increasing mobility of the population, together with the increasing proportion of older persons in the population, has focused attention on the geographic mobility of the aged population.

It is important to study the mobility of the older age groups because older persons do move in substantial numbers, and this movement, coupled with the trend towards an increasing percentage of older persons in the population, has the potential for creating high concentrations of the elderly in selected regions of the country. Such concentrations have important implications regarding the demand for and the supply of a wide variety of services, ranging from housing to recreation, to health care and social services. Further, concentrations of older persons have economic implications, both good and problematic, at the local, provincial and national levels, and raise questions of regional equity. For example, if the elderly population should concentrate disproportionately in British Columbia, and given that per capita health care costs are higher for the older age groups, then British Columbia might argue that federal contributions to its health care budget should be adjusted upwards to reflect the province's relatively top-heavy age structure. In short, the geographic mobility of the older population, in conjunction with increasing proportions of older persons in the population, has important policy implications. For this reason, both the population aging trend and the patterns of geographic relocation of the older population merit serious attention.

The term "the elderly," as used above, refers to those who are fifty-five years of age and older. While this monograph primarily focuses on the "elderly" population, that is on persons sixty-five years of age and older, it would be a mistake to completely ignore the near-elderly age group. Further, the fifty-five and older age group is by no means homogeneous, and the discussion and analysis that follow often make explicit comparisons. For example, the near-elderly aged fifty-five to sixty-four and the younger-elderly aged sixty-five to seventy-four might be contrasted with the older-elderly seventy-five or more years of age.

It is important not to stereotype the various elderly age groups, because there are no clear dividing lines. For example, retirement, which may precipitate a change of residence, may come at age sixty-five, but often comes either earlier or later. Disability, resulting from declining health, may precipitate a move and may come early for some, later for others, and not at all for the remainder. Similarly, widowhood or loss of financial independence may precipitate moves at various ages. Further, voluntary moves reflecting preferential choices may be undertaken at any time in the later years. Nevertheless, both the likelihood of moving and the type of move undertaken are age related. Retirement moves tend to occur near the age of sixty-five. Voluntary moves designed to improve the quality of life are more frequently undertaken by the near-elderly and the younger-elderly age groups rather than by the older-elderly. Forced moves occasioned by loss of independence tend to come in the later years. Consequently, this monograph examines mobility patterns focusing on the older years from age fifty-five onwards, with special attention paid to the various elderly age categories, especially sixty-five to seventy-four and seventy-five and older.

This monograph focuses primarily on Canada. While interest in the geographic mobility of elderly populations began to rise in the 1970s in countries such as Britain, France, and the United States, interest has been more recent in countries such as Australia and Canada. The literature of all these countries is reviewed briefly, focusing on comparisons and contrasts with Canada.

This mongraph is intended for a wide variety of readers, including lay persons, undergraduate students, and professionals in both government, academia, and the private sector. So as to reach as wide an audience as possible, the analysis is primarily descriptive, and statistics are presented in the form of percentages and simple rates, for example, the number of movers for every thousand persons. Multivariate analyses and complex models are not attempted in this volume, although it is anticipated that the materials presented in the following chapters might stimulate those endeavours.

The structure of the book is as follows. Chapter 1 presents a brief introduction. Chapter 2 reviews the various concepts and theoretical approaches used in the discussion of geographic mobility. In addition, this chapter presents a typology identifying the various kinds of older adult mobility and compares and contrasts elderly and non-elderly movement patterns and motivations. Finally, Chapter 2 examines the research literature that focuses on the movement of elderly Canadians and examines the sources and limitations of available data.

Chapter 3 presents an analysis of the geographic mobility of the elderly in Canada, based primarily on 1981 census data and on address changes in the mailing lists of Old Age Security recipients. This chapter examines local movement patterns, intraprovincial and interprovincial migration, and international moves. Further, this chapter compares patterns of elderly mobility for different geographic areas (Canada as a whole, the provinces individually, and each of the largest cities), and also analyzes variations in mobility patterns dependent on the characteristics of individual movers (that is, ethnicity, socio-economic status, marital status, gender, and age). Finally, Chapter 3 examines the patterns of interregional migration to assess the extent to which the elderly population is being geographically redistributed and concentrated in selected locales.

Chapter 4 discusses mobility across the life span, examining the relationship between the tendency to move and the mover's age and position in the life cycle. This chapter reviews relevant literature and also analyzes data from the 1981 Census, showing the relationship between age and the probability of making a move of a given nature (local, intraprovincial, or interprovincial). Finally, Chapter 4 examines the lifetime migration patterns of those Canadians who were sixty-five and older in 1981, and also compares the mobility patterns of elderly persons at the time of the 1961, 1971, 1976, and 1981 censuses. This final analysis addresses the question: "Are the elderly increasingly likely to move?"

Chapter 5 discusses the mobility patterns of the elderly populations in the United States, Britain, France, and Australia. Comparisons and contrasts with Canada are made, and implications for future migration patterns in Canada are examined. Chapter 6 discusses the implications for elderly mobility of Canadian policies in the areas of retirement, Old Age Security, health care insurance, housing, and immigration. Further, Chapter 6 examines how elderly mobility patterns influence Canadian policy. Finally, Chapter 7 presents a summary and discussion, and identifies unanswered questions for future research.

ACKNOWLEDGEMENTS

I am grateful to the Social Sciences and Humanities Research Council for a leave fellowship in 1982–83 which helped me to explore issues in the demography of population aging. I am also grateful to Professor Barry McPherson who subsequently noted my work on the migration of the elderly in Canada and invited me to write this monograph for the Butterworths Perspectives on Individual and Population Aging series. As editor of this series, Professor McPherson provided me with both opportunity and helpful editorial suggestions. I also wish to thank Janet Turner and the staff at Butterworths (including Lebby Hines, Linda Kee, and Lori Newlands) for their marvellous support. Over the two years that this project unfolded, I received regular letters from Butterworths reminding me of impending deadlines. These letters cost me a little sleep, but, nevertheless, reassured me of Butterworths complete and professional commitment to this project. I am also grateful to Susan McKellar at Health and Welfare Canada who provided me with the Old Age Security data (summaries of address changes) and helpful information. The University of Alberta, as always, provided a superlative environment for academic research. The University of Alberta Faculty of Arts Grants Committee facilitated my work by releasing me from some of my teaching duties during January–April 1987. The Department of Sociology at the University of Alberta provided research assistants and support ranging from photocopying to typing. I am especially grateful to Judy Mitchell, Shirley Stawynchy, and Val Irwin who typed the entire manuscript. Cameron Stout and A. K. M. Nurun Nabi helped with library research and Nabi assisted with figures 3.1 and 4.1 and suggested figure 3.2. Professor Carl Grindstaff reviewed the entire manuscript and provided helpful suggestions and encouragement, both of which were very much appreciated. Finally, I am grateful to my family (Laura, Ryan, Jennifer, and Melissa) who provide the justification for all of the time spent behind my desk.

CONTENTS

TABLES

FIGURES

CHAPTER 1

INTRODUCTION

Canada has experienced a multitude of changes in the twentieth century. Canada has grown in population from five million to over twenty-five million residents since the beginning of the century. Immigrants have arrived in great numbers from Europe and more recently from "Third World" countries. The Prairies have been settled, the mountains crossed, and the northern frontiers explored. Great cities — notably Montreal, Toronto and Vancouver — have become major world centres. Furthermore, this growth in the Canadian population during the twentieth century has been accompanied by improvements in the life expectancy of individual Canadians. The acute infectious diseases have been largely conquered by modern sanitation and by modern medicine. Consequently, child mortality has dropped. In addition, modern medicine has reduced the risks of childbearing, and maternal mortality has declined substantially. Today, the majority of Canadians live more than their biblical three score and ten years.

In addition to population growth and increasing life expectancy, Canada has experienced substantial change in other areas. For example, Canada's economy has shifted emphasis from agriculture to industry to services. Industrialization and post-industrialization have meant that our population resides increasingly in cities rather than in rural locations. Furthermore, technological changes have been rapid, and one single generation living in Canada's twentieth century has plowed a farm field walking behind a team of horses, driven an automobile, and flown in an airplane. In other words, Canadians have enjoyed a rising standard of living.

At the same time that life expectancies and living standards have reached their current high levels, birth rates have reached dramatic lows. The decreasing rate at which young people are added to the population coupled with the increasing rate of survival into old age means that there are relatively more old people and relatively fewer young people in Canada's total population. The twentieth century has seen the percentage of Canadians aged sixty-five and older increase from 5 percent in 1901 to almost 10 percent as of the 1981 Census (see McDaniel 1986 for a detailed discussion of the demographics of population aging in Canada). By 2031, it is projected that the elderly portion of the population will approach 25 percent,

1

unless there is a return to patterns of high fertility (Denton et al. 1986; McDaniel 1986, 106).

In addition, the twentieth century has witnessed the institutionalization of retirement such that the great majority of Canada's elderly withdraw or are excluded from the labour force. The twentieth century has also witnessed the emergence of the Canadian welfare state with Old Age Security and universal hospital and medical care insurance. These policies have served to create, outside of the labour force, a relatively large population which has guaranteed minimum incomes and which is largely protected from the financial burdens of health care costs.

In short, Canada has an increasingly large number of elderly persons who make up a substantial and growing percentage of the population and who often enjoy both good health and reasonable wealth. Such a population — elderly, retired, healthy or with access to health care, and with adequate economic means — enjoys considerable opportunity to reside where it chooses. The question, then, is: Where do Canada's elderly (choose to) reside?

The popular media, and oftentimes our relatives and acquaintances, make us aware of the attraction that the American Sunbelt states such as Florida, California and Arizona present for both elderly Americans and elderly Canadians (some of whom journey to these destinations for the winter months only — hence the designation "snowbirds"). Further, the demographic literature speaks of the "graying" of parts of Europe as a consequence of elderly in-migration (Cribier 1980, 261).[1] Finally, within Canada, southern Ontario, British Columbia, and especially the city of Victoria, for example, are considered to be our sunbelt retirement magnets. In other words, the phenomenon of migration in the later years has become increasingly notable and widespread in both Europe and North America.

The graying of certain geographic locales raises a number of questions. For example, what are the effects of concentrations of elderly persons on local economies? What are the implications for housing supply and demand (that is, for private houses, private apartments, retirement communities, subsidized housing and old age homes)? What are the implications for medical care, hospital services, and nursing homes, and for community and social services (including, for example, recreation facilities, libraries, and senior citizen centres)? The concern behind these questions can be illustrated, in the extreme, by considering an absurd scenario. Assume that all Canada's elderly are motivated to escape hostile winters and that every Canadian, upon reaching retirement age, picks up and moves to British Columbia — to the Okanagan or to Vancouver or to Victoria. Now, given that hospital and medical care are primarily provincial responsibilities (although the federal government helps pay the bills, and often establishes policy with which the provinces are "invited" to comply), and given that the elderly make disproportionate demands on hospitals, nursing homes, and medical care services, the concentration of the elderly in British Columbia would mean that that province alone would have to bear the burden not only of housing but also of providing medical care for every elderly person in Canada. Under these circumstances, one would expect the province of British Columbia to demand policy changes so that the other provinces and the federal government would more "equitably" share in the economic costs of providing services to the elderly. Do not assume, however, that British Columbia would necessarily be opposed to this heavy influx of elderly persons. The elderly would bring life savings, pensions, Old Age Security cheques and so on, thereby infusing funds into local economies. The elderly, as consumers, would stimulate certain sectors in the market place, would create jobs and, for the most part, would not require or take jobs for themselves. Further, as mentioned above, the presence of the elderly might be used to justify demands for transfers of public revenues into British Columbia. In short, the graying of British Columbia might be a burden in some respects, a blessing in others. Indeed, Barry McPherson (personal communication, 6 April 1986) notes that the in-migration of the elderly might be encouraged as a form of tourism development in order to attract resources to a given region.

Geographical movement of the elderly has been largely ignored by those studying migration. The great bulk of migrants have been young to middle-aged adults who move primarily for economic reasons. Historically, the elderly have represented only a small percentage of the population and an even smaller percentage of migrants; consequently, elderly migration has been largely neglected by demographers and other researchers. However, with the aging of the population, that is, with the increase in the percentage of the population that is elderly, and with the tendency for the elderly to move to selected locations, attention has recently begun to focus on elderly migration and its consequences. The purposes of this monograph are (1) to review what is known about elderly migration in Canada, (2) to analyze and explain available Canadian data, primarily census data pertaining to migration, (3) to comment on the implications of Canadian policies for elderly migration and, vice versa, on the implications of elderly migration for Canadian policies, and (4) to identify unanswered research and policy questions.

NOTE

1. Note that "graying" also occurs when younger persons move out of an area leaving elderly persons behind.

CHAPTER 2

GEOGRAPHIC MOBILITY: CONCEPTS, TYPOLOGIES AND THEORIES

This chapter reviews the concepts and theories of geographic mobility and develops a typology of elderly movers. The mobility of older Canadians is compared and contrasted with non-elderly movement and an explanatory model is developed. Finally, the Canadian research literature is reviewed, and the sources and limitations of available data are discussed.

CONCEPTS OF GEOGRAPHIC MOBILITY

Geographic mobility involves physical movement, that is, a change in the place of residence. Geographic mobility should not be confused with social mobility which refers to a change in social status, whether vertical change up or down in the social hierarchy or horizontal change within the same hierarchy level. Geographic mobility may be permanent or temporary. (An illustration of temporary, that is, seasonal, mobility, for example, is elderly persons, "snowbirds," from Toronto or Winnipeg spending the winter in Florida.) Permanent changes of residence are often local moves covering a relatively short distance and staying within some significant geopolitical boundary. Movers who cross this geopolitical boundary are designated "migrants" (as opposed to the "non-migrant" local movers). Note that the factor which distinguishes migrants from non-migrants is not the distance of the move per se, but rather the crossing of a boundary chosen to define migration. Some migrants may relocate at very short distances across that boundary while some local movers may relocate at more substantial distances without crossing the critical boundary. Nevertheless, migrants generally move greater distances than non-migrants.

Migration may be "internal," that is, within a given country, or "external" (that is, international), crossing national boundaries. It follows that an elderly person moving from Manitoba ("origin") to British Columbia ("destination") is an internal migrant within Canada, an "out-migrant" from Manitoba, and an "in-migrant" to British Columbia. An elderly person moving permanently from Winnipeg to Sun City, Arizona is an international (external) migrant, an "emigrant" from Canada, and an "immigrant" to the United States.

5

A large number of migrants, who over a given period of time, move from one particular origin to a particular destination constitute a migration "stream." For example, there is a fairly substantial stream of elderly migrants leaving the Prairie Provinces for British Columbia. Strong streams such as this, however, tend to develop "counterstreams." For example, there is a modest counterflow of elderly migrants moving from British Columbia to the Prairie Provinces. A significant portion of such a counterflow involves elderly persons "returning" home. The difference between in-migrants and out-migrants (or between immigrants and emigrants) is referred to as "net" migration and indicates the total gain or loss of population due to the migration process.

The Canadian Census is a major source of data on the "mobility status" of Canadians. The Census adapts the concepts discussed above by defining a mover (in contrast to a non-mover) as a person whose usual place of residence on Census Day is different from that person's usual place of residence five years previous. Hence, the Census records a person's "five-year mobility status." Movers are divided into non-migrants (local movers) and migrants, that is, persons who move from one census subdivision (for example, city, municipality, county) to another. Internal migrants are those who migrate within Canada while external migrants are persons who move to or from Canada. Note that a person who is sixty-five years of age at the time of a given Census and who is classified as a mover, changed residence at least once during the previous five years. That is, this person moved during his or her sixtieth to sixty-fifth year . The exact timing of the move is not recorded. Finally, the difference between the number of persons moving to and moving from a given location over a five-year period defines net migration.

The terminology used in discussions of geographic mobility (see Nam and Philliber 1984, 170–72) is summarized below:

    I. Temporary (Seasonal,
       Circulatory) Mobility .... Vacationers, "Snowbirds"
   II. Permanent Mobility...................... Movers, Migrants
       A. Local Mobility .... Non-migrants/Local Movers
       B. Migration .... Migrants
          1. Internal Migration .... Out-migrants (from origin)
                                          In-migrants (to destination)
                                                      Net gain or loss
          2. External (International)
             Migration.................... Emigrants (from origin)
                                         Immigrants (to destination)
                                                      Net gain or loss

THEORIES OF MOBILITY

The discipline of demography has been criticized for being atheoretical, and while there have been countless studies of mobility/migration and its correlates, there have been few attempts to formulate explicit theories (Lee 1966, 48). The first attempt to define "The Laws of Migration" came from Ravenstein in 1885 and 1889. Ravenstein (see Lee 1966, 48) noted several generalizations including: the economy plays a primary role in determining migration (for example, the push of rural economies, the pull of urban commercial and industrial centres, and the desire of people for material betterment); distance tends to deter migration (that is, most moves are of short distance); and major currents (streams) of migration tend to produce countercurrents (counterstreams). While the elderly often migrate for non-economic reasons, Ravenstein's observations on distance and on stream-counterstream still apply to the patterns of migration of contemporary older Canadians.

The next most significant formulation of a theory of migration was attempted by Lee (1966) more than three-quarters of a century after Ravenstein. Lee defines migration as any permanent or semi-permanent, voluntary or involuntary change of residence, regardless of the distance moved.[1] Lee argues that the mobility/migration decision and process is influenced by factors associated with: the area of origin, the area of destination, intervening obstacles, and the personal aspects of the potential or actual mover. Factors associated with the origin and destination take the form of pushes (which tend to repel a person from either the place of origin or a potential destination) or pulls (factors which tend to hold a person at the place of origin and which tend to attract a potential migrant to a given destination).

Lee argues that the nature of a given factor is subjectively assessed; that is, one person might perceive a given factor negatively, another might perceive that same factor positively, while a third might react indifferently. Though groups of similar individuals will tend to have similar perceptions of origin and destination factors, nevertheless, the assessment of factors remains an individual, subjective judgement.

There are important differences in the subjective assessment of origin and destination factors: people tend to have more complete and more certain information about the origin than about the destination. Further, people, especially as they age, tend to develop sentimental attachments to the place of origin, and also may, initially at least, experience a certain dislocation or culture shock upon moving to some new destination. Both sentimental attachments and culture shock tend to colour perceptions and may give the origin a positive hue, while the destination, initially at least, may be viewed with a certain apprehension.

According to Lee, the decision to move depends not only on the subjective evaluation of origin and destination pushes and pulls, but also on the subjective assessment of intervening obstacles. These include the distance and cost of the move, physical barriers such as a mountain range or an ocean, and legal and political barriers such as a national boundary. In any case, the individual decision to move requires that the assessment of origin and destination pluses and minuses, and of intervening obstacles, must be sufficient to overcome "the natural inertia which always exists" (Lee 1966, 51). The subjective assessment of factors also depends on "impedimenta" such as a spouse and children, and on personal factors such as intelligence, personality (for example, whether conservative or adventurous), and stage in life cycle (starting a career, getting married, having children growing up and leaving home, retiring). Lee (1966, 51) notes that the decision to migrate is "never completely rational" nor is the decision necessarily personal or democratic; that is, parental decisions affect young children, the employed spouse may make a migration decision for the entire family, or an employer might make a decision to transfer an employee (and therefore the employee's family).

Lee's general formulation applies equally well to both non-elderly and elderly migration, although these two groups will tend to respond differently to given push and pull factors. Employment-related economic factors are more important to the non-elderly; non-economic variables will tend to be more salient for the elderly.

Lee (1966, 52–57; for a critique, see Goldscheider 1971, 50–75, especially 53–54, 58, 65–66, 71) goes on to develop specific hypotheses relating to the volume of migration, the development of migration streams and counterstreams, and the personal characteristics of migrants. Lee's hypotheses are generalizations relating to the general population of movers, the majority of whom are non-elderly. Further, some of these hypotheses, especially those that relate to the volume of migration, focus on economic–labour market opportunity which is more salient for the non-elderly than for the elderly. In short, not all of Lee's hypotheses apply to elderly migration. Those hypotheses which can be applied to the volume of elderly migration (Lee 1966, 53–54) suggest that: the volume of migration is inversely related to the barriers intervening between origin and destination; and volumes and rates of migration tend to increase over time with rising standards of living and with the increasing ease of communication and transportation. Further, migration leads to migration. That is, migrants make it easier for other people to migrate by providing information and contact at the destination and, in addition, previous migrants themselves are more likely to become migrants again at some future time. In other words, in modern societies, successive generations tend to develop increasingly mobile life-styles.

Hypotheses relevant to the formation of elderly migration streams and counterstreams include (Lee 1966, 54–56): (1) streams of migrants to highly specific destinations (for example, Victoria, St. Catharines) tend to develop, and are reinforced as earlier migrants send back information and recruit others to follow; (2) every major migration stream tends to develop a counterstream as some migrants will return for a variety of reasons including disenchantment or disappointment with the new living arrangements or changes in economic factors in the receiving area such as increases in the cost of living or, for emigrants from Canada, declines in the value of the Canadian dollar. Further, changes in health or changes in economic status may encourage a return move in order to gain the support of persons or familiar surroundings "back home"; (3) the difference between stream and counterstream, that is, net migration, will be high in favour of the destination if negative factors at the origin (for example, cold Prairie winters) are positive factors at the destination (for example, British Columbia's mild winters and early springs); (4) conversely, net migration will be low if origins and destinations are very similar, with the consequence that migration streams will tend to be nearly equalled by counterstreams (for example, net exchanges of the elderly between the Atlantic Provinces); and (5) net migration will tend to be high if intervening barriers are significant. For example, migrants travelling great distances may be reluctant to return because of the heavy investment that they have made in migrating, because of the cost of returning, and so on.

Finally, hypotheses relating to the characteristics of elderly migrants include (Lee 1966, 56–57): (1) migrants tend to be selected groups and not a random sample of the population (for example, the poor or the wealthy); (2) migrants drawn to a destination by its positive features tend to be the more advantaged members of the population, that is, wealthier, healthier, more educated, more experienced in terms of past mobility, and so on; and (3) persons at certain stages of the life cycle (for example, children leaving home, retirees, those who have lost a spouse) have an increased tendency to move.

In short, Lee's general push-pull formulation and a number of his specific hypotheses apply to elderly migration. Indeed, Lee's 1966 article remains one of the most significant of recent attempts to delineate a general "theory of migration."

In 1976, Ritchey assessed the status of migration theory for the second *Annual Review of Sociology* by focussing on the causes of migration (excluding local mobility). He (see also Shaw 1975) discussed migration studies under three headings: labour mobility studies which are largely economic in nature and often focus on the economic characteristics of groups and/or communities; social demographic studies which focus on a wide variety of individual characteristics; and cognitive-behavioural approaches which emphasize the subjective aspects (as opposed to the objective economic or socio-demographic aspects) of migration decision making.

The labour mobility studies are largely irrelevant for the elderly who tend to be retired and/or less concerned with economic employment issues, unless, of course, the elderly migrant's move is motivated by a non-elderly migrant — an adult offspring, for example. Ritchey (1976, 373) does note that distance is often introduced as a barrier to economically motivated migration, and distance would also seem to be a barrier to (non-economically motivated) migration in the later years.

The social demographic approaches to migration are more applicable to the elderly than are the labour mobility studies. The social demographic studies (Ritchey 1976, 378) tend to examine the relationship between migration and the individual's place in the social structure, including such indicators as the individual's social class (income, occupation, education), racial and/or ethnic status, gender, age, position in the life cycle, and family and community ties. In addition, the social demographic studies also tend to take social-psychological variables into account by examining individual motivations, expectations, aspirations, attitudes, values, and perceptions. Inasmuch as the social demographic studies tend to emphasize factors which attract and repel the individual, this approach, therefore, tends to utilize a push-pull framework.[2] Lee's 1966 theory of migration, discussed earlier, exemplifies this push-pull social demographic approach to migration.

Ritchey (1976, 395–97) suggests that within the social demographic approach there are three general and overlapping perspectives which may explain the migrant's decision-making process. One approach views the decision to migrate as a cost-benefit analysis in which the advantages and disadvantages of moving or not moving, and of this place or that place, are weighed. This cost-benefit analysis examines both tangible economic costs and benefits as well as the more subjective psychological advantages and disadvantages. A second approach — the adjustment-to-stress approach — sees migration as an attempt to cope with problems and dissatisfactions attending life in a given locale (for example, neighbourhood deterioration, urban crime, and the like). At some point, the distressed individual or family begins to consider relocation as a means of coping. A third approach notes that potential migrants may have rather different individual "modes of orientation," with one making decisions in a coldly rational fashion, while another uses emotionally hedonistic criteria or acts on the basis of long-established habit. These various, although interrelated, perspectives on the process of migration decision making apply equally well to both elderly and non-elderly persons.

In addition to the labour market and social demographic approaches, Ritchey (1976, 397–98) briefly discusses the cognitive behavourial approach to migration phenomena. This approach emphasizes the subjective preferences people have and share for various locations. The perceived attractiveness of various areas can then be ranked, relatively, according to the consensus of opinion. In Canada, for example, one would anticipate that elderly Canadians would rank British Columbia and southern Ontario as highly desirable locations and would put Saskatchewan and Newfoundland well down on the list of preferences. Further, these preference rankings are expected to correlate with actual migration patterns. Of course, an elderly person who rates British Columbia as highly attractive might or might not move there. The preferential ranking, however, is thought to predispose the choice of British Columbia as a destination should migration actually take place.

The effects of distance on migration have been observed ever since Ravenstein noted this factor over one hundred years ago. A recent study by McLeod et al. (1984) shows that the "gravity model" (see Zipf 1946) constitutes a significant explanation for the interstate migration of persons fifty-five and older in the United States. In short, the volume of a given elderly migration stream is a positive function of the size of the elderly population at both the origin and destination and is a negative function of the distance between the origin and destination. In other words, two large populations will tend to exchange a large flow of migrants, although this flow will diminish with increasing distance. In the Canadian context, one would expect larger exchanges of elderly persons between Quebec and Ontario than between Manitoba and Saskatchewan, simply because Quebec and Ontario have significantly larger populations. The exchange between Ontario and British Columbia relative to the exchange between Alberta and British Columbia will be increased by Ontario's larger size but will be decreased by Ontario's greater distance from British Columbia. Of course, other factors in addition to distance also influence the volume of migration exchange (McLeod et al. 1984).

A TYPOLOGY OF ELDERLY MOBILITY PATTERNS

Residential moves undertaken by older adults may be voluntary or involuntary, local or non-local, and permanent or temporary.

Voluntary Versus Involuntary Moves

Sell (1983, 301–04) discusses "a volitional typology of reasons for moving." Sell identifies three types of mobility: forced (involuntary) moves, imposed changes of residence, and preference-dominated (free or voluntary) moves. "Forced" mobility occurs when circumstances completely override individual preference and require that an individual move. Examples of such compelling circumstances include natural disasters such as flood or earthquake and personal disasters such as loss of health resulting from a stroke or loss of income resulting from termination of employment or death of a provider. As persons enter retirement age and the loss of income that often results, the likelihood of a forced move increases. Further, increasing age is associated with an increased risk of health problems that may compromise the ability to live independently. Health crises or declines often force a temporary move into a hospital and/or a longer term move into a nursing home or a relative's home where care can be provided. In addition to personal and natural disasters, examples of circumstances which override individual preference include public policy decisions such as destruction of existing housing in an urban renewal project, regulations governing eligibility for public housing, and private owner-management decisions to convert apartment buildings into condominiums or otherwise terminate rental housing agreements. As an illustration of the last point, during Expo 86 in Vancouver, it was alleged that many renters (including many low-income elderly persons) were forced out of their living quarters in order to accommodate the anticipated influx of short-term visitors who would be willing to pay significantly higher rental fees.

According to Sell, "imposed" mobility differs from forced mobility mainly in the degree of coercion. Imposed mobility occurs when other persons make the decison, leaving little freedom of opportunity for decision making on the part of the person forced to move. Or at least, the individual is "forced to decide" and often accepts the recommended course of action. For example, the family that an elderly person lives with and is dependent on moves because of a job transfer, or a nursing home decides that a client needs a greater or lesser level of care and recommends that the patient be moved accordingly. In both cases the elderly person is forced to make a decision to move, and while there are alternatives to be considered, these tend to be limited, and pressure is often exerted so that the person chooses some alternative strongly recommended by others.

Sell distinguishes imposed from forced mobility by arguing that, for forced mobility, failure to move leads to life-threatening consequences or results in the mobilization of agents of social control, such as the police, who guarantee the move. Imposed mobility can be resisted with less dire consequences; nevertheless, both imposed and forced mobility are alike in that there is a significant lack of freedom to make a voluntary "perference-dominated" choice.

In sharp contrast to forced and imposed mobility, Sell describes preference-dominated mobility as a freely chosen course of action taken by individuals acting on their personal evaluation of pushes and pulls. Examples of preference-dominated mobility include a voluntary move to a better neighbourhood or to a more desirable climate or a move back to the region of one's birth or childhood.

Local Versus Non-local Moves

Besides varying in the degree of constraint (that is, forced or preference-dominated), mobility varies in terms of the distance of the move. Most moves are local in nature and are, therefore, of short distance. Non-local intraprovincial and interprovincial moves decrease in likelihood with increasing distance. Nevertheless, whether the distance moved is short or long, moves are undertaken for various reasons and can be classified according to both the distance of the move and the motivation for the move.

In an attempt to delineate the various types of moves undertaken by the elderly, Cribier (1980, 257–59) discusses "five types of aged residential mobility." She first focuses on the older worker who voluntarily moves some distance for job-related reasons, or alternatively, who takes employment in a place in which approaching retirement is desired (preretirement migration). Cribier next discusses retirement migration which involves moves (usually of long distance) made by persons who have retired from the labour force. Most of these moves occur soon after retirement, and most of the movers, therefore, are the younger elderly. Most retirement moves are preference-dominated and follow years of planning and anticipation.[3] Cribier (1975, 363–64) notes that retirement migrants tend to be either return migrants — returning to their region of origin — or "amenity" seekers drawn to some attractive place. Amenity migration is an increasingly important phenomenon. An amenity is an attractive or desirable feature of a place such as a pleasant climate, or a pool, tennis courts, sauna, security, et cetera. The migration of elderly persons from the American Snowbelt to the Sunbelt, the migration of elderly Canadians from the Prairies to British Columbia, and the seasonal winter migration of older Canadians to Florida or Arizona are all examples of amenity-drawn migration patterns.

In contrast to the voluntary and highly valued, long-distance preretirement or retirement move, Cribier's third type of residential mobility focuses on forced or imposed moves that are negatively valued and often of short distance. These moves are the result of the aging process and the associated declines in health and/or economic status that lead to increased frailty and dependency. People making these forced or imposed moves tend to be the older elderly or the prematurely disabled. Institutionalization, for example, a move into an extended care hospital or nursing home, is typical of such a move.

Cribier's first three types of moves are motivated by either retirement or dependency. Cribier's fourth type of mobility is motivated by neither of these factors, per se, but rather refers to moves that are undertaken voluntarily for whatever reason of choice (other than the advent of retirement or dependency). These moves tend to be local in nature and are often motivated by a desire for a better neighbourhood or for better housing.

While Cribier's first four categories of moves focus on various types of permanent mobility, her fifth type of mobility concerns temporary and seasonal moves in later life. These moves often cover considerable distance and last considerably longer than a normal vacation. Examples include "snowbirds" who spend the winter in Florida or Arizona or persons who spend the summer on the coast or at the lake.

Wiseman and Roseman (1979; see also Wiseman 1980) also present a typology of the mobile elderly which focuses on different kinds of local and non-local moves. The Wiseman and Roseman typology is based on the motivations that influence elderly persons as they contemplate the possibility of moving or staying and as they contemplate possible destinations. With respect to the decision to move or not, these authors note the importance of life cycle transitions which serve as "triggering mechanisms" sufficient to override "inertial" ties and lead to a decision to migrate. Such triggering mechanisms include children leaving home, retirement, death of spouse, and loss of independence. In addition to the triggering mechanisms, two other factors — "environmental stress" and rising standards of living — play important roles in overcoming residential inertia to precipitate a change of residence. Rising standards of living suggest that more and more elderly have the financial means to afford a move. Environmental stress refers to the decline in neighbourhood quality as housing stock ages and deteriorates, as housing units are converted into rental units with accompanying increases in the "transient" population, as crime rates rise, and so on. These increasing environmental stresses lead to growing residential dissatisfaction and, at some point, may lead to a decision to move.

The decision regarding where to move, whether from one house to another, or from a house to an apartment, or from an apartment to an institution, may be either forced or free. That is, the choice of destination depends on whether one is moving to gain assistance or amenities. Increasing dependence may force a person to decide to move into an institutional setting. The choice of institution will depend on such factors as the availability of facilities, or eligibility criteria, and/or on ability to pay. On the other hand, many decisions to move are relatively free choices, and the destination chosen depends more on personal preferences, on the location of family members and friends, for example, and on information people have gained about potential destinations through their own prior travels, from friends and relatives, and/or from the media.

Having discussed the decision-making process generally, Wiseman and Roseman (1979) develop a typology of local and non-local mobility for elderly movers. These authors introduce six types of local mobility (suburbanization, apartmentalization, inner-city relocation, communalization, homes of kin, institutionalization) and three categories of longer-distance migration (amenity, return, and kinship migration).

The first type of local moves, suburbanization (and related exurbanization), involves the movement of healthier and wealthier (middle-class and upwards) elderly residents of larger cities to the more attractive nearby suburbs, rural fringes, and satellite towns. Indeed, such movement of elderly persons has played a part in the recent growth of many non-metropolitan areas in the United States following decades of decline (that is, the rural-urban turnaround) (Heaton et al. 1981).

Wiseman and Roseman's second type of local moves, apartmentalization, is common among the healthy and financially secure elderly couples and widows who move locally in order to downsize and simplify their housing so as to reduce the burden of upkeep and/or to facilitate travel plans. While Wiseman and Roseman are thinking primarily of private-sector apartments, in Canada, government-subsidized apartments are also available for the independent elderly and tend to attract the older, often widowed, person of limited financial means.

The poorer elderly and, in particular, the poorer, never-married and widowed elderly often rent inexpensive accommodation in the inner city. Included in this third category are persons who have long been "chronic movers," that is, persons who have moved repeatedly from one inexpensive rental unit to another mostly within the inner city. Also included in this group are persons who rent single rooms (single-room occupancies) in old rooming houses and old hotels. These inner-city elderly have a tendency to relocate within the central city.

Wiseman and Roseman's fourth category, communalization, involves a move into multi-unit housing where certain activities such as dining are shared. In Alberta, for example, and in other Canadian provinces, senior citizen "lodges" illustrate such a housing option. Typically, people who move into communal housing are the older, often widowed, elderly who have had their independence compromised due to declining health and/or finances. While communalization is a form of institutionalization (discussed separately below), persons moving into communal settings are relatively less dependent than are those persons moving into nursing homes or extended care hospitals.

Another alternative for the older, widowed dependent elderly who need some assistance is to move in with, or at least, move nearer to family members, usually an adult offspring and his or her spouse and children. For example, a widowed woman moves in with her daughter, son-in-law, and grandchildren. For the dependent elderly person, however, both communalization and institutionalization provide alternatives to living with kin.

Institutionalization is Wiseman and Roseman's final category of local moves. Those elderly in poor health, usually the older elderly, are at increased risk for a forced or imposed move into an extended care hospital or nursing home.

While the great majority of elderly moves are local moves, nevertheless, there is also a significant movement of the elderly across longer distances. Wiseman and Roseman discuss three types of elderly migration: amenity, return, and kinship migration.

Amenity migration is usually undertaken at the time of retirement, hence, in Cribier's (1980) terms, it is also a kind of retirement migration. Such a move usually involves the relatively healthy and financially well-off younger elderly couple.

Wiseman and Roseman's second type of longer-distance moves is referred to as return migration. Because the twentieth century has seen a great migration of persons from rural settings to urban environments, many of today's elderly have rural origins, and there is a tendency for these elderly to return to towns in their home regions. Like amenity migration, such moves tend to take place shortly following withdrawal from the labour force and under such circumstances are also, therefore, a type of retirement migration.

Wiseman and Roseman's third and final type of elderly long-distance mobility is kinship migration. Younger elderly couples in favourable circumstances may move from one city to another to be near their grown children and grandchildren. Such moves resemble amenity-drawn retirement migration. Further, older, often widowed, elderly in need of or in anticipation of need of assistance may move to be near or, less often, may move in with geographically distant family members.

Permanent Versus Temporary Moves

Wiseman and Roseman's (1979) typology of local and non-local moves (discussed above) focuses on permanent moves. Cribier (1980) notes that the phenomenon of elderly migration includes temporary seasonal moves as well as permanent moves. Elderly Canadians may spend the summer at the cottage or may winter in Palm Springs, or both. Indeed, among the healthy and financially secure elderly, the percentage of persons engaging in regular temporary migrations may far exceed the percentage of elderly who engage in permanent long-distance migration. These temporary seasonal migrations are an increasingly common part of the life of many elderly Canadians; nevertheless, little is known about the frequency, duration, distance, destination, and consequences of this migratory pattern. The implications of seasonal migration are discussed later in Chapter 6.

ELDERLY VERSUS NON-ELDERLY MOBILITY: SIMILARITIES AND DIFFERENCES

Geographic mobility is age related. Mobility rates show a distinct peak in the young adult years and a dramatic decline for the middle- and elderly-age groups (see Chapter 4). Age implies position in the life cycle, and young adulthood is the time for a number of life-cycle transitions including graduation from high school, going to college, leaving home, starting a career, getting married, and starting a family. All of these transitions have a tendency to be accompanied by geographic mobility. In contrast, in the middle years, job security, home ownership, and the demands of raising a family tend to be associated with residential stability. In the later years, life-cycle transitions such as children leaving home, retirement, death of a spouse, and loss of independence may be accompanied by some degree of geographic mobility. Nevertheless, residential inertia built up over an adult lifetime tends to be strong, and elderly mobility rates are substantially less than non-elderly mobility rates. In short, elderly and non-elderly mobility are alike in that both tend to be associated with life-cycle transitions. They are different in that mobility is less likely in the elderly years than in the non-elderly years. Moreover, the life-cycle transitions triggering a move are very different for young and old Canadians. The young are entering the labour force and starting their own family. The elderly are retiring from the labour force, and their family members are beginning to disperse and, perhaps, die. Transitions for the young adult imply increasing inde-pendence and responsibility. For the elderly, life-cycle transitions such as children leaving home or retirement imply increased freedom; however, events such as loss of a spouse or loss of health imply increasing depen-dence. In short, life-cycle transitions are associated with mobility for both age categories; however, the life-cycle events triggering a move by an older person are very different from those motivating a younger person's move, and the consequences for subsequent life-styles are quite different.

It has long been argued that economic factors play a central role in the process of geographic mobility. This is particularly true for the majority of migrants, that is, younger adults, who frequently move to find employ-ment, to advance their careers, or to enhance their socio-economic status. Elderly mobility is distinctly different in that changes of residence are more likely to accompany withdrawal from the labour force and more likely to be influenced by other non-economic considerations such as quality-of-life issues or health (Wiseman and Roseman 1979, 325).

While the elderly may be influenced differently from the non-elderly by economic employment factors (Serow 1987), nevertheless, other economic factors do play a part in both elderly and non-elderly mobility. The cost of moving and the cost of living in various regions, for example, are important considerations for both elderly and non-elderly alike (Murphy 1979, 85–86; Serow et al. 1986).

The majority of the elderly are retired from economic employment and are therefore, resources permitting, free to move for life-style reasons. It follows that the salience of non-economic factors is a main difference be-tween elderly and non-elderly mobility. Just the same, studies exploring the migration turnaround in the United States (the reversal in the decades-long pattern of net movement from non-metropolitan to metropolitan contexts) suggest that non-economic "quality-of-life" considerations are becoming increasingly important determinants of migration for both the elderly and the non-elderly (Williams and Sofranko 1979; Murdock et al. 1984; Heaton et al. 1981). In other words, while non-economic quality-of-life factors have tended to be more influential for elderly migrants than for non-elderly migrants, it appears that these quality-of life considerations are becoming increasingly important for both the elderly and the non-elderly alike.

A SOCIAL DEMOGRAPHIC MODEL OF ELDERLY MOBILITY

It would appear that a social demographic model similar to that proposed by Lee (1966) will provide a better explanation of elderly mobility than will a model which primarily emphasizes economic factors. Figure 2.1 presents such a model.

Figure 2.1 illustrates four specific relationships between the objective and subjective determinants of mobility and the actual act of changing residence. First, objective variables such as age, social class, distance, and the push and pull of unattractive and attractive features all have a direct effect on the propensity to make a move of a given type or to a given destination (arrow one). For example, turning age sixty-five increases the likelihood of a person making a life-style–oriented move, especially if that person is of a higher social class. Objective variables also have an indirect effect on mobility (arrows two and three) in that objective variables predict certain subjective variables (arrow two), and subjective variables, in turn, predict mobility (arrow three). For example, the social class or the quality of the neighbourhood lived in influences a person's attitudes, expectations, perceptions, and so on. In turn, these subjective variables influence the propensity to move.

Arrows two and three suggest that the objective and subjective variables combine additively to predict mobility. Arrow four, however, implies that the objective and subjective factors may also combine interactively to predict mobility; that is, the effect of objective factors on mobility may depend, in part, on certain subjective variables. For example, the effect of the objective variable "presence of kin" may depend on the extent to which a person subjectively values familial relationships. For a person who values family connections highly, the presence of kin at the origin is likely to be a strong deterrent to mobility, while the presence of kin at a potential destination will be a strong attractive force predisposing migration. On the other hand, for a person who does not value familial ties, the presence of kin will be largely irrelevant having little or no effect on the tendency to either move or stay.

In summary, objective factors have both direct effects and indirect effects (operating through the subjective factors) on the tendency to change one's residence. Further, subjective factors have direct effects on mobility and also may interact with objective factors to influence the nature of the relationships between objective factors and mobility. Finally, this model focuses on the individual, examining a person's objective and subjective

FIGURE 2.1

A SOCIAL DEMOGRAPHIC MODEL OF ELDERLY MOBILITY

SUBJECTIVE FACTORS

1. Psychological Variables
   attitudes, values,
   aspirations, expectations,
   evaluations, perceptions,
   and so on.

2. Decision-Making Processes
   cost-benefit,
   place utility,
   residential satisfaction,
   and so on.

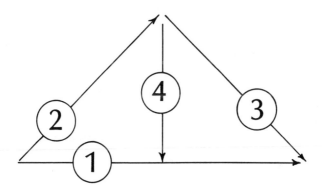

OBJECTIVE FACTORS

1. Personal Variables
   age, sex,
   social class, ethnicity,
   marital status,
   position in life cycle,
   mobility history and experience,
   health, and so on.

2. Origin and Destination Variables
   neighbourhood quality,
   presence of kin and/or friends,
   access to services and amenities,
   and so on.

3. Intervening Variables
   distance, cost,
   and so on.

MOBILITY

1. Move of a Given Type
   temporary, permanent,
   voluntary, forced,
   local, intraprovincial,
   interprovincial, international,
   retirement, amenity,
   return, and the like.

2. Move to a Given Destination
   for example, British Columbia or
   southern Ontario.

characteristics and circumstances, and tendency to make a move of a given type or to a given place. This model could be recast to focus on the group by examining the social demographic characteristics of groups or communities and their effect on the volume of migration streams. Generally, however, the social demographic model will rely on individual-level data obtained from sample surveys. Such survey data have been relatively rare in Canada to date, although the Census does provide individual-level data on some of the variables in the model (for example, personal characteristics such as age, sex, marital status, social class, and mobility status including whether the person moved or not and, for movers, the origin and destination and therefore distance of the move).

A REVIEW OF THE RESEARCH LITERATURE ON THE GEOGRAPHIC MOBILITY OF OLDER CANADIANS

Migration in the Canadian context has been extensively studied (see, for example, Courchene 1974, 1970; George 1970; Grant and Joseph 1983; Grant and Vanderkamp 1986, 1984, 1976; Kalbach 1970; Lycan 1969; Marr et al. 1978, 1977; McInnis 1971; Pooler 1987; Shaw 1985; Shulman and Drass 1979; Simmons 1980; Stone 1979, 1978, 1969; Trovato and Halli 1983; Vanderkamp 1968; and Winer and Gauthier 1982).

The primary focus of these studies has been on the non-elderly (who constitute the bulk of movers) or on the general population. Therefore, little, if any, systematic attention has been devoted to the analysis of the phenomenon of elderly migration. Those studies that do examine the migration of the elderly are less common and tend to be of more recent vintage, that is, since the early to mid-1980s. The following review of literature examines the geographic mobility patterns of the elderly in Canada.

One of the earliest Canadian studies of elderly mobility is Golant's (1972) analysis of census data for the 1956–61 period, and of survey data collected in 1964 providing information on changes of residence (and also daily trip activity) of older (late middle-aged and elderly) Torontonians. Golant (1972, 58–60) observes that the elderly are less likely to move than are the non-elderly, that most moves are of relatively short distance, and that, while elderly females (many of whom are widowed) tend to be more mobile than elderly males (many of whom are married), nevertheless, elderly females are less likely to move long distances. Further, Golant (1972, 67) observes that while the fringe areas of the greater Toronto Census Metropolitan Area experienced net in-migration of older persons, the City of Toronto had a net out-migration to smaller centres and to rural areas. Nevertheless, there is substantial residential stability among the elderly, especially among those who are married and who are homeowners. When the elderly do move, there is a strong tendency to move into apartments or other multiple-family dwelling units (Golant 1972, 94–97, 109).

Shulman (1980, 32–33) reports on interprovincial migration from a 1978 unpublished study by Rowe and Pong that was based on Old Age Security and census data. This study found that while the elderly are less likely to move than the non-elderly, nevertheless, the patterns of elderly and non-elderly migration in terms of provinces of origin and destination are quite similar. Further, this study found some evidence for a retirement-age peak in mobility rates and for a pattern of return migration. Finally, it was noted that British Columbia experienced by far the highest rate of net migration gain while Saskatchewan experienced the highest net loss.

Connidis (1983) asked a representative sample of elderly persons living in their own homes in London, Ontario, whether they would like to live with one of their children or in a facility for seniors, assuming that circumstances changed such that the elderly person could no longer live independently. Of course, the question is hypothetical, and Connidis did not study actual mobility.

Connidis found that the great majority of the elderly (who were not already living with children and who had children with whom they might live) preferred to live in a facility for the elderly rather than with their off-spring. This preference was even more pronounced for elderly females than for elderly males. However, Connidis (1983, 365) notes that:

> Reasons given for choosing a facility for seniors tend to be negative rather than positive. The majority of respondents phrase their comments in terms of the reasons for *not* living with children rather than the reasons *for* living in a facility. This suggests that the choice of a facility is subject much more to push rather than pull pressures; that is, respondents don't typically choose facilities because of their perceived attractive features but instead, for a variety of push factors related to perceived problems involved in living with children. (Emphasis is in the original.)

For example, the elderly often explained their choice of a facility in terms of not wanting to be a burden, not wanting to interfere, or in terms of perceptions that living with their grown children would be unfair to them and their families, or simply would not work due to inherent conflicts between the generations and their respective needs and life-styles. While these are reasons for choosing *not* to live with offspring, on a more positive note, a frequently stated reason for wanting to live in a facility was the desire to preserve a measure of independence and to have privacy, quiet and the company of people who were of similar age.[4] Even this theme, though, reflects the disadvantages of living with offspring. In short, the majority of elderly would choose to live in a facility, not because the facility is attractive, but rather because living with their children was perceived to have drawbacks.

A minority of respondents — males more than females — did say that they would choose to live with their children. Over 40 percent of the reasons given for this choice emphasized the positive aspects of extended-family living. On the other hand, over 20 percent chose family living because of the problems that they perceived with senior citizen facilities. Almost 30 percent were ambivalent, saying, for example, that they would prefer to live with family but would not want to become a burden. In short, only a minority preferred to move in with their children rather than to move into a facility, and even fewer of the elderly made this choice because of a clear-cut perception of the advantages of family living. The great majority of the elderly perceive the tensions and problems of multi-generational living, and, while life in a facility is not the "ideal" choice, most see it as the best practical solution once circumstances prevent the individual from living independently.

While Connidis examined hypothetical forced moves, Liaw and Nagnur (1985) examine actual out-migration from Canada's metropolitan and non-metropolitan regions.[5] Liaw and Nagnur used the 1971–76 Census data and explicitly focused on the relationship between migration and age. With respect to elderly migration, these authors employed a model which predicts an increased mobility potential around the age of retirement. Liaw and Nagnur (1985, 87) note that females, over the course of their lives, tend to be more mobile than males, this being true for short-distance moves although not for interprovincial moves. Further, these authors (1985, 91–100) note a slight increase in the tendency to migrate near the age of retirement, with this weak "retirement peak" in out-migration rates coming at 60.5 years of age for females and at 63.5 years of age for males for all regions combined (the sex difference being largely a function of the age difference between spouses). However, the residents of Canada's non-metropolitan areas and smaller urban centres did not exhibit an increased tendency to out-migrate near the age of retirement. On the other hand, there was evidence of increased out-migration near the age of retirement for both males and females living in the three largest urban centres — Toronto, Montreal, and Vancouver — with Vancouver having the lowest out-migration rate of the three. In other words, retirees living in Vancouver are less likely to move away from that city and are more likely to "age in place."

Liaw and Kanaroglou (1985) further developed the Liaw and Nagnur (1985) analysis discussed above. While the previously discussed paper examines all ages and both sexes, the Liaw and Kanaroglou paper focuses specifically on elderly (55–79 years of age) male out-migrants from Canada's cities in the 1971–76 period. These latter authors report that retirement migration often occurs before the age of sixty-five and that elderly male migrants, in comparison to non-elderly males, are more likely to select a non-metropolitan destination. For those elderly males migrating from one city to another, characteristics such as distance, cultural dissimilarity between origin and destination, coldness of climate, and high cost of living (rent) tend to discourage choice, while a warm climate exerts a strong pull.

Cheung and Liaw (1986) arrived at similar findings for elderly female out-migrants from Canada's cities in the 1971–76 period.

While the Liaw and Kanaroglou and the Cheung and Liaw papers discussed above use aggregate (community-level) data, Ledent and Liaw (1986) present an analysis of micro (individual-level) data which examines elderly (sixty-five years of age and older) migration in Canada in the 1976–81 period. They observe that the elderly population's tendency to migrate decreases with age, decreasing faster for males than for females. Moreover, elderly persons not residing in the province of their birth are more likely to migrate than elderly persons residing in their province of birth; the married elderly are less mobile than the non-married, with the divorced and separated being the most mobile; elderly males who are retired from the labour force are more mobile than the employed; elderly couples without children present in the home are more mobile than elderly persons who have children present; and the better educated are more mobile than are the less educated. Further, higher income inhibits migration before retirement but promotes migration after retirement. Finally, male and female out-migration rates are very similar. With respect to the destination chosen (that is, whether this move is local in nature, intraprovincial, or interprovincial), the older elderly (seventy-five or more years of age) are slightly more likely than the younger elderly (sixty-five to seventy-four) to move short distances; those elderly who are not currently resident in their province of birth are more likely to move interprovincially; Francophones are less likely to move interprovincially; the better educated and those with higher incomes are more likely to move to another province; and, retired couples with no children present in the home are more likely to move longer distances. Ledent and Liaw (1986, 50, 53) observe that, because elderly persons who are not living in their province of birth have a tendency to "return home," the migration process differs somewhat from elderly persons already living in their province of birth. This suggests that there is a significant "return migration" phenomenon that is distinct from other forms of elderly migration.

An analysis of the mobility of several cohorts of elderly Canadians, using data from the 1961, 1971, 1976, and 1981 Censuses, indicates that the elderly are increasingly likely to move from one province to another, and that this movement of elderly persons, while partially offset by the movement of the non-elderly, nevertheless, affects the provincial concentrations of older persons (Northcott 1985; 1984a). That is, the proportion of elderly persons in a province tends to rise when elderly in-migration rates exceed non-elderly in-migration and, conversely, when non-elderly out-migration rates exceed elderly out-migration. For example, the proportion of British Columbia's population that is elderly is elevated by the heavy in-migration of elderly persons (despite the partially counterbalancing effect of non-elderly in-migration) while Saskatchewan's proportion of elderly residents is elevated by the heavy out-migration of the non-elderly (despite the partially counterbalancing effect of elderly out-migration). In short, while interprovincial migration affects provincial age structures, the similarity of elderly and non-elderly migration streams in Canada tends to moderate these effects. Should elderly and non-elderly migration streams become more distinct, then more dramatic concentrations of elderly persons in certain provinces would soon emerge.

Finally, turning to elderly migration between Canada and the United States, Sullivan and Stevens (1982) report that in a travel trailer park (in November of 1980) and in a mobile home park (in March of 1981) in the East Mesa–Apache Junction area of Arizona, 12 percent and 20 percent of residents respectively were from Canada. In February of 1986, Marshall and his colleagues (see Marshall and Longino 1987; Tucker et al. 1987) mailed questionnaires to the 4,500 subscribers of the Florida-based English-language newspaper, *Canada News*. Over 90 percent of these subscribers were older Canadians, largely from Ontario; and 59 percent responded to the survey, including 1,976 persons sixty-five years of age and older. While the respondents to this questionnaire constitute a convenience sample (that is, they are not necessarily representative of older Canadians wintering in Florida — Francophone Canadians, for example, are greatly underrepresented), nevertheless, this is the largest survey of Canadian snowbirds wintering in the United States known to the author to date (and the only survey devoted exclusively to Canadians). This survey found that the Canadian snowbirds wintering in Florida were predominantly married, healthy, and middle to upper-middle class. Further, many of these seasonal residents had vacationed in Florida previously before buying a mobile home, condominium, or single-family home in Florida, and many had "a long history of progressively more lengthy visits to Florida" (Tucker et al. 1987, 11). Indeed, fully three-quarters of the survey respondents owned accommodation in Florida, almost as many as owned accommodation in Canada. Further, Marshall and Longino (1987, 7–8; see also Tucker et al. 1987, 10) observed that a significant percentage of these snowbirds seemed to own two vacation homes — one in Ontario (for example, in the summer cottage country north of Toronto) and one in Florida — and thereby could be classed as "perpetual vacationers." Finally, Marshall and his colleagues report that somewhere between one-quarter and one-half million elderly (mostly eastern) Canadians visit Florida each year and that many of them stay in Florida for a substantial period of time, that is, they are "seasonal residents" rather than "visitors." Indeed, the average length of stay for respondents to the survey was five months. Note that this study does not examine the seasonal migration of western Canadian snowbirds, the majority of whom are thought to winter in Arizona and California. In other words, Marshall and his colleagues highlight the magnitude and importance of the phenomenon of elderly seasonal migration and the need for further research into this topic.

SOURCES OF DATA ON THE GEOGRAPHIC MOBILITY OF OLDER CANADIANS

In order to obtain a complete and accurate picture of the mobility of Canada's older citizens, ideally one would interview each and every mover (or at least a representative sample), identifying both current and previous residences and inquiring as to the motivations and circumstances of the moves. Thus, one could analyze the various kinds of geographic mobility; for example, a researcher could distinguish return migration, retirement migration, forced movement for reasons of economy and/or health, and so on. In practice, such a survey would be very expensive, very time consuming, and would require a complete listing of all recent movers. While such a study is certainly possible (a listing of elderly movers might be obtained from address changes to the Old Age Security mailing list providing that confidentiality could be guaranteed), nevertheless, for this present monograph no attempt is made to obtain new data. Instead, available data are used to describe recent patterns of geographic mobility of older Canadians.

The largest and most accessible set of data on geographic mobility in Canada is the Canadian Census. Information on mobility was first collected for the 1961 Census when one in every five residents of Canada (aged five years or more) was asked the question, "Where did you live five years ago?" The same question was asked of one in every three Canadian residents for the 1971 and 1976 Censuses, and in 1981 and 1986 that question was once again addressed to a one-in-five sample (data for 1986 were not available at the time of writing).[6]

The data collected in the Census are available in various formats. Basic tables and cross-tabulations are printed in a series of publications. More detailed tables, known as User Summary Tape files, are available on microfiche and/or on computer tape. For persons who wish to construct their own tables, raw census data are available for 1981, 1976, and 1971 on the Public Use Sample Tapes (PUST). These data files are created by choosing representative samples from respondents to the long-form census questionnaire. In 1981, one in every ten individuals who answered the long form were selected for the user sample. Given that the long form went to one in five residents of Canada, it follows that the PUST individual file constitutes a one in fifty, that is, 2 percent sample ($\frac{1}{10} \times \frac{1}{5} = \frac{1}{50}$). There is also a PUST household/family file, which is a 1 percent sample containing data on census family units and on "non-family" persons, that is, persons who did not live in a family unit.

In addition to census data, information on changes in residence for Canada's elderly could be obtained from lists that contain the addresses of persons identified by age. For example, Revenue Canada maintains a file containing a 10 percent sample of taxpayers. Furthermore, virtually all residents of Canada are registered for provincial health care. Alternatively, information on the address changes of the elderly could be obtained from lists that contain elderly persons only; for example, all elderly persons (except recent immigrants) receive Old Age Security benefits.

Based on Old Age Security address listings and changes of address, Health and Welfare Canada provided summary tables indicating moves as well as the average yearly number of Old Age Security (OAS) recipients for 1971 through 1985. OAS recipients include all elderly residents of Canada and elderly persons living outside of the country who lived at least twenty years in Canada after turning eighteen years of age or who have departed within the past six months. This latter category may contain persons who leave Canada for the winter and who then return. In short, the data provided by Health and Welfare Canada record the average number of persons paid both inside and outside of the country each year. Further, these data also record the yearly total of intraprovincial moves (within a province from one postal code to another) as well as the total number of interprovincial moves for each year. (The number of moves per hundred OAS recipients is calculated by dividing the number of moves by the average number of recipients and then multiplying by one hundred.)

LIMITATIONS OF EXISTING DATA SOURCES

The Census aims to obtain a response from every person who is resident in Canada on Census Day. It is, of course, possible that some individuals will be missed altogether or counted more than once. Undercoverage is far more likely than overcoverage, and it has been estimated that for the 1976 and 1971 Censuses, the overall undercoverage rate is about 2 percent, with this percentage being higher for certain subpopulations such as young males or recent immigrants (The Census of Canada 1981, VIII).

With respect to the data obtained from the five-year mobility question (that is, "Where did you live five years ago?"), limitations include (see, Ledent and Liaw 1986, 7; George 1970, 9–12; Northcott 1984a, 5; Statistics Canada, no date): (1) the characteristics of movers are recorded at the time of the Census rather than at the time of the move (which may be up to five years earlier), consequently, the link between mover characteristics and the propensity to move is obscured somewhat; (2) should a person move several times in the five-year period, only one move — the change from the first to the last residence is counted; (3) should a person move and then return to the original residence within the five-year period, then no move is counted; (4) should a person die or emigrate from Canada, then such persons are not available to respond to the current Census, and their data are lost; (5) there is sampling error for the 20 percent long-form sample and for the 2 percent Public Use Sample — this error is larger for small numbers, for example, elderly interprovincial migrants to or from a small province; and finally, (6) while persons who have been institutionalized in collective dwellings (for example, hospitals, nursing homes, old age homes) for six months or more are counted, detailed information, including information on mobility status is not recorded. In other words, persons institutionalized for longer than six months appear in the 100 percent data set but are excluded from the more detailed 20 percent and 2 percent samples. Table 2.1 presents a comparison of the number of elderly persons recorded in the 100 percent, 20 percent and 2 percent samples.

Table 2.1 reveals that the 20 percent and 2 percent samples contain mobility data on virtually all persons fifty-five to sixty-four years of age; indeed, less than 1 percent of this age group are excluded. However, for those persons sixty-five years of age and over, there is a discrepancy of some 7.5 percent between the 100 percent sample on the one hand and the smaller samples on the other hand. The actual numbers of persons excluded in the 20 percent and 2 percent samples are almost identical to the number of persons counted as inmates of institutional collective dwellings (for example, inmates of hospitals and nursing, chronic care and old age homes). You will recall that persons institutionalized for more than six months preceding the Census are excluded from the 20 percent sample (and therefore from the 2 percent sample). This practice appears to be the primary explanation for the discrepancies between the various census data sets.

Table 2.2 shows that the percentage of persons excluded from the detailed 2 percent sample rises exponentially with age, doubling approximately every five years. That is, while less than 2 percent of persons aged sixty-five to sixty-nine are institutionalized and therefore excluded from the mobility data, over 35 percent of persons aged eighty-five or more are lost to the analysis.

TABLE 2.1

A COMPARISON OF THE NUMBER OF ELDERLY RECORDED IN THE 100 PERCENT, 20 PERCENT AND 2 PERCENT CENSUS SAMPLES, BY AGE, FOR 1981

Age	100% Sample	20% Sample	Difference	Inmates of Institutional Collective Dwellings[1]	Missing Data 2% Sample[2]
55–64	2,159,230	2,141,930	17,300 (0.8%)	17,675	18,450
65+	2,360,980	2,184,550	176,430 (7.5%)	173,035	176,950

1. Includes hospitals and nursing, chronic care, and old age homes.

2. This is the number of persons for which mobility information is unavailable, as estimated from the 2% Public Use Sample.

SOURCE: Statistics Canada, The 1981 Census of Canada, Volume 1, Catalogue Numbers 92–901 (Table 1), 92–903 (Table 1) and 92–907 (Table 1); and the Public Use Sample Tape (2 percent sample).

TABLE 2.2

PERCENTAGES OF ELDERLY FOR WHICH MOBILITY DATA ARE UNAVAILABLE, BY AGE, ACCORDING TO THE 1981 CENSUS 2 PERCENT PUBLIC USE SAMPLE

Age	Percent Excluded from the 2 Percent Sample[1]
55–59	0.7
60–64	1.1
65–69	1.8
70–74	3.3
75–79	7.3
80–84	15.8
85+	35.5
55+	4.3
65+	7.5

1. Those excluded, for the most part, are inmates of institutional collective dwellings such as hospitals and nursing, chronic care, and old age homes.

SOURCE: 1981 Public Use Sample Tape (2 percent sample), The 1981 Census of Canada.

In short, mobility data for those persons who are institutionalized during the six months or more preceding the Census are not available. While only about 7.5 percent of all elderly are thereby excluded (and even smaller percentages of the younger elderly), nevertheless, rather substantial percentages of the oldest elderly (eighty years of age and more) are lost to the analysis. This means that the Census mobility data underrepresent the geographic mobility of the older elderly and, in particular, underestimate moves into institutional settings — moves which are often forced by circumstances of declining health. This exclusion of the institutionalized elderly is a major limitation of this analysis and suggests that there is a need for a separate focused examination of moves to and from institutions.

Another estimate of the extent to which the Census undercounts actual moves is provided by the 1971 Census. In 1971, the following question was asked: "How many times have you MOVED from one Canadian city, town, village, or municipality to another since June 1, 1966?" (Moving away and then returning to the same place was counted as two moves; persons coming to Canada did not count their arrival as a move but did count subsequent moves within Canada. These data, then, record intraprovincial and interprovincial migration, but do not count local moves within a given municipal boundary.) First of all, these data show that 87 percent of all elderly Canadians did not move across a municipal boundary between 1966 and 1971. On the other hand, the five-year mobility question (that compares present residence with residence of five years previous) indicates that

90 percent made no moves. This latter question fails to count multiple moves and counts a person who leaves and returns as a non-mover. In other words, the widely used five-year mobility question overestimates the number of non-movers. The reciprocal side of these data, of course, is that instead of counting 13 percent as migrants, the five-year mobility question counts only 10 percent. Second, these data show that, on the average from 1966–1971, every 100 movers made at least 153 moves. More specifically, for every 100 persons who moved, 68 made one move, while 20 made 2 moves and another 6, 2 and 3 persons made 3, 4, and 5 or more moves respectively. Overall, census data (the 5-year mobility question) underestimate both the number of movers and the number of moves.

In contrast to the census data, the Old Age Security data include all elderly recipients of OAS cheques including those persons who are institutionalized. Inasmuch as the census data exclude the institutionalized, this completeness is an advantage of the OAS data. Further, while census data count immigrants but exclude emigrants, the OAS data does the reverse, excluding recent in-migrants but counting OAS recipients abroad. However, the OAS data are not broken down by age or sex or by any other variable — this facility being a major advantage of the census data. Further, the OAS data (and also the census data) cannot be used to identify the type of move, that is, whether the move is forced or voluntary, motivated by retirement and life-style considerations or by a desire to return home, and so on. On the other hand, an advantage of the OAS data is that all moves are counted — the census data record only whether a person's present address is the same or different five years ago. The OAS data record multiple moves and return moves, both of which are lost in five-year census mobility data. However, the OAS data do not allow for the identification of individual mobility patterns. That is, there is no indication as to how many persons move once in a given period as opposed to those who move several times or who do not move at all. A final advantage of the OAS data is that these data are available one month after a change of address is processed, while census data on moves up to five years previous are available only after another eighteen months or so. Nevertheless, the recorded date of move for the OAS data is the date that the administrative action took place, not the actual date of move (which could be up to several months prior to the administrative action). Further, intraprovincial changes of address include only moves from one postal code to another. If a person's postal code remained unchanged, then his or her move would not be recorded (McKellar, personal communication 1986). (For a comparison of OAS, census, and income tax data, see Statistics Canada, no date.)

The OAS data and the census data each provide different, and incomplete, pictures of elderly mobility. The census data identify those persons who are currently sixty-five and older and who moved at least once in the past five years. (Note that these movers — five years previously — were sixty years of age and older.) The OAS data record moves of persons sixty-five years of age and older only. In other words, while the census data identify *movers*, the OAS data count *moves*. Table 2.3 compares these two data sources and their distinct pictures of mobility. This table shows that the number of *movers* per hundred elderly persons is substantially less than the number of *moves* per hundred elderly persons. A focus on movers (the census data) underestimates the total amount of movement, while a focus on moves (the OAS data) overestimates the proportion of movers.

NOTES

1. Note that earlier in this chapter, the term "migration" was applied to longer-distance moves across a significant geopolitical boundary; Lee's definition corresponds to the concept of general geographic mobility including both local moves and longer-distance migrations.
2. Ritchey (1976, 389) discusses several interrelated hypotheses which examine the push-pull nature of community and kinship ties and which are germane for elderly migration. The "affinity" hypothesis argues that the presence of friends and relatives at the place of origin serves as an

TABLE 2.3

A COMPARISON OF MOBILITY DATA FROM TWO DIFFERENT SOURCES, FOR PERSONS SIXTY-FIVE YEARS OF AGE AND OLDER, FOR 1976–81

Source	Intraprovincial Moves	Interprovincial Moves
Public Use (2%) Sample Number of elderly movers (persons who moved at least once), per 100 elderly[1]	22.5	1.78
Address Changes for Old Age Security Recipients Number of moves, per 100 elderly[2]	54.0	2.80

1. Excludes the institutionalized. Calculated according to following formula:

$$\frac{\text{number of persons aged 65+ in 1981 who moved at least once during June 1, 1976 to June 1, 1981}}{\text{number of persons aged 65+ on June 1, 1981}} \times 100$$

2. Includes the institutionalized. The number of address changes in a given year (April 1 to March 31) times 100 divided by the average monthly number of Old Age Security recipients for that year. Rates for 1976, 1977, 1978, 1979, and 1980 were then summed. The rate of intraprovincial moves for 1976 was obtained by extrapolation of the 1977–1980 pattern.

SOURCE: These data are derived from data presented in greater detail in Tables 3.1 and 3.4.

inertial factor tending to prevent migration, while the presence of friends and relatives at the potential destination serves as an attracting magnet drawing migrants. The "information" hypothesis suggests that friends and relatives at a potential destination act as sources of information about the distant location and play a role in the decision to migrate. The "facilitating" hypothesis argues that friends and relatives at the destination offer material and/or psychological support, thereby facilitating the migration process.

3. Note that a distinction can be made between retired persons who move for whatever reason and retired persons who are motivated to move specifically by the event of retirement. This distinction is not always maintained, and the term "retirement migration" has been applied to both the movement of retired persons generally and to those who move because of retirement per se.

4. Wister (1985) also emphasizes the value that elderly persons place on independence and privacy.

5. The metropolitan centres studied by Liaw and Nagnur (1985) are known as Census Metropolitan Areas (CMA's) and are defined by Statistics Canada (1982:97) as a labour market area with an urbanized core of 100,000 or more population.

6. You might recall that all residents of Canada are required to respond to the Census. The majority fill out a short form which does not ask about mobility. A minority — 20 percent or 33 percent, depending on the census year — fill out the long form, including the question on change in residence.

Because the 1986 census data on the geographic mobility of the 20 percent sample were not available at the time of writing, this analysis focuses on the 1981 and earlier Censuses. More specifically, the 1981 census long form, sent to 20 percent of the population, asked, "Where did you live five years ago on June 1, 1976?" and the respondent was asked to check one of the following: "This dwelling; Different dwelling in this city, town, village, borough, or municipality; Outside Canada; Different city, town, village, borough, or municipality in Canada (specify below)." Spaces were provided so that the respondent could indicate the place of previous residence. A separate question also asked, "How long have you lived in this dwelling? Less than one year, One to two years, Three to five years, Six to ten years, More than ten years." In addition, the 1981 Census asked, "Where were you born?" and the respondent accordingly indicated the province or territory in Canada or the country outside of Canada where he or she was born. Finally, immigrants to Canada were asked, "In what year did you first immigrate to Canada?" In contrast to the 1981 Census, in 1976 residents were asked only the one question, that is, "Where did you live 5 years ago, on June 1, 1971?" Response categories were the same as for 1981.

The geographic mobility questions asked on the 1971 Census (long form; 33 percent sample) parallel those on the 1981 Census, but include one additional question. The additional item on the 1971 Census was: "How many times have you MOVED from one Canadian city, town, village or municipality to another since June 1, 1966? *Count moving away and returning to the same place as 2 moves.* None, 1, 2, 3, 4, 5 or more" (emphasis in original). This is a useful question in that the five-year mobility item ("Where did you live 5 years ago?") counts multiple moves as 1 move only and fails to count moves when the person returns home within the five-year period.

There were no mobility questions asked on the 1966 Census, and 1961 marked the first year in which the five-year mobility question appeared. In that Census the five-year mobility question was asked of a 20 percent sample of persons fifteen years of age and over. (For persons five to fourteen years of age, mobility status was assumed to be the same as the family head. Persons under five, of course, did not have a residence five years previous.) In addition, the 20 percent sample of all residents was asked, "How long have you lived in this dwelling?" while everyone was asked about their province or country of birth and date of immigration, if applicable.

CHAPTER 3

THE GEOGRAPHIC MOBILITY
OF OLDER CANADIANS

This chapter explores the recent patterns of geographic mobility of older Canadians using census data for the 1976–1981 period and using address changes to the Old Age Security recipient lists for the 1971–1985 period.

Table 3.1 reports the average numbers of Old Age Security recipients for 1971 to 1985 together with the numbers of intraprovincial moves (changes of postal code) and interprovincial changes of address. Note that these data report the number of moves rather than the number of movers. (Inasmuch as one mover may make more than one move, these data overestimate the actual number of movers.)

Table 3.1 shows that the numbers of intraprovincial changes in postal code from 1977 to 1985 have tended to fluctuate at about ten to eleven moves per hundred Old Age Security recipients per year. In addition, the numbers of interprovincial moves from 1971 to 1985 have fluctuated around 0.5 moves per hundred, that is, five moves per thousand elderly each year. In other words (assuming that persons who move, move but once in a given year), over 10 percent of the elderly population change their place of residence each year. Moves are more likely to be of short rather than long distance; indeed, in any given year there are some twenty intra-provincial moves for every one move across a provincial boundary.

Finally, Table 3.1 provides a rare glimpse into elderly migration out of Canada. Elderly persons who leave Canada for less than six months,[1] and elderly persons who have emigrated (at any age) after being resident in Canada for at least twenty years of their adult lives, are eligible for OAS payments. In 1977, the Old Age Security Act was amended to provide for the payment of partial OAS pensions and to provide for inclusion of OAS pensions in reciprocal international social security agreements (Health and Welfare 1984, 13.6–13.7). Partly as a result of these policy changes, since 1979, there has been a steady increase in both the numbers and in the pro-portion of OAS payments made to persons living outside of Canada. In 1985, 1.4 percent of all OAS cheques were sent to persons residing outside of the country. In December of 1985, 37,328 OAS cheques (totalling $8,389,930) were mailed to persons outside of Canada. Two-thirds of these payments went to the United States, 9 percent to Italy, 7.5 percent to the United Kingdom, and one-sixth to all other countries.

TABLE 3.1

INTRAPROVINCIAL AND INTERPROVINCIAL CHANGES OF ADDRESS AND PERSONS PAID OUTSIDE OF CANADA, FOR OLD AGE SECURITY RECIPIENTS, 1971–85

Year[1]	Number of Recipients[2] (000's)	Intraprovincial Changes of Address[3]		Interprovincial Changes of Address[4]		Persons Paid Outside of Canada[2]	
		(000's)	(per 100)	(000's)	(per 100)	(000's)	(%)
1971	1,746	—	—	8.0	0.46	15	0.85
1972	1,791	—	—	9.2	0.52	15	0.83
1973	1,838	—	—	9.5	0.52	15	0.82
1974	1,888	—	—	7.8	0.41	15	0.79
1975	1,936	—	—	9.1	0.47	14	0.72
1976	1,989	—	—	10.3	0.52	14	0.70
1977	2,051	230	11.2	12.4	0.61	14	0.67
1978	2,116	228	10.8	13.8	0.65	13	0.60
1979	2,201	234	10.6	11.7	0.53	24	1.08
1980	2,276	228	10.0	11.1	0.49	27	1.20
1981	2,342	255	10.9	10.7	0.46	29	1.25
1982	2,404	243	10.1	11.2	0.46	31	1.29
1983	2,464	247	10.0	11.6	0.47	33	1.34
1984	2,529	248	9.8	13.7	0.54	35	1.37
1985[5]	2,615	302	11.5	14.7	0.56	37	1.40

1. Fiscal year — April 1 to March 31 of the following year.
2. Monthly average.
3. Change of postal code. Yearly totals. Data not available 1971–1976.
4. Yearly totals.
5. Estimate for year based on data for first nine months.
SOURCE: Adapted from Income Security Programs Statistics, Health and Welfare Canada.

PATTERNS OF MOBILITY BY AGE AND SEX

One of the advantages of the census data, in contrast to the OAS information, is that census data can be classified according to various socio-demographic variables. For example, Table 3.2 indicates the number of years that men and women in the older age categories have lived in their current residence. This table shows that over one-half of all older Canadians have lived in their current residence for over ten years. Note that the OAS data discussed above suggested that some 10 percent of the elderly population moves each year (assuming one move per person per year). If one simply summed this statistic over ten years, one might reach the conclusion that, on the average, 100 percent of the elderly population move each decade. However, such a computation assumes that each elderly person moves once and only once in that decade. The census data clearly show that such assumptions are erroneous. The census data show that a majority of the elderly population is stationary for long periods of time. In other words, there are likely three groups of elderly: those who have not moved in some time, those who have moved once, and those who have made multiple moves. Indeed, any given person in a course of a lifetime may move from one category to another, for example, breaking a period of long-term residence with a period of high mobility.

Returning to Table 3.2, while more than one-half of the elderly have lived in their current residence for over ten years, elderly males are somewhat more likely than elderly females to be long-term residents, indicating that elderly females are somewhat more mobile. Further, those persons seventy-five years of age and older are most likely to claim long-term residency, indicating that the younger elderly are somewhat more likely to move than are the older elderly. However, these data probably understate the mobility of the older elderly. Institutionalized persons are not included in this data set and, therefore, health-related moves into institutions are excluded. Because the older elderly are most likely to be involved in such moves, their mobility is underestimated. The higher mobility of the younger elderly may also be a function of age-related events such as retirement and the tendency for younger-birth cohorts to be increasingly mobile.

While the preceding discussion emphasizes length of residency, that is, the tendency *not* to move, the following discussion focuses on the tendency to move. Table 3.3 shows that more than one in every four males sixty-five to sixty-nine years of age changed their place of residence at least once during the five-year period from 1976–1981. Table 3.3 also reveals that the tendency to move declines somewhat with increasing age, dropping to one mover for every five males eighty-five or more years of age.[2] The pattern for elderly females is similar to that of elderly males except that elderly

TABLE 3.2

NUMBER OF YEARS IN CURRENT DWELLING, BY AGE AND SEX

Length of Occupancy (years)	Males (%)			Females (%)		
	55–64	65–74	75+	55–64	65–74	75+
Less than 1	6.5	5.7	4.4	6.6	6.1	4.9
1–2	8.7	8.5	6.9	9.9	9.5	8.0
3–5	13.2	14.2	12.0	14.0	15.5	13.4
6–10	15.3	15.2	14.3	15.1	16.2	16.3
More than 10	56.4	56.4	62.3	54.4	52.8	57.3
Total[1]	100.1	100.0	99.9	100.0	100.1	99.9

1. Differences from 100.0 are due to rounding error.
SOURCE: The 1981 Public Use Sample Tape (2 percent sample), The 1981 Census of Canada.

females at any given age are somewhat more likely than elderly males of the same age to change their place of residence.

Local Moves

While there is a considerable degree of movement among older people of all ages, the majority of moves are local in nature and do not involve a change of city, town, village or municipality. With increasing age, the general trend for older males is a modest decline in the probability of a local move. Females aged fifty-five and older peak in local mobility at ages sixty-five to sixty-nine and subsequently, with increasing age, show a modest decline in the tendency to move short distances. Finally, older females at any given age are more likely than their male peers to move locally.

Non-local Moves Within the Same Province

Very generally, older people are about one-half as likely to move across a municipal boundary — staying, nevertheless, within the same province — as they are to move locally within the same municipality. The probability of these longer-distance intraprovincial moves peaks at ages sixty-five to sixty-nine for elderly men and at ages sixty to sixty-four for older women. Thereafter, mobility rates tend to decline modestly with increasing age. The ages at which these peaks occur suggest they are in part motivated by retirement. Of course, many of these older men and women are married to each other and move together as one unit. Given that men tend to be older than their wives, the female migration rate peaks at a slightly younger age than the male rate.

Interprovincial Moves

Moves from one province to another are relatively infrequent among the older population (aged fifty-five and older). The probability of interprovincial migration peaks at ages sixty to sixty-nine for older males and at ages sixty to sixty-four for elderly females, and declines with increasing age. Again, the pattern suggests that retirement is a precipitating factor in interprovincial migration leading to peak rates at retirement age. Overall, in 1981, some 1.8 percent of those persons sixty-five years and older (more than 39,000 elderly persons — about the population of a medium-sized city) had changed their province of residence at some time between 1976 and 1981 (Northcott 1985, 188). However, given that these elderly migrants are moving to various provinces, and given that some are returning to their province of origin, it must be emphasized that the interprovincial migration of less than two in every hundred elderly persons in a given five-year period does not indicate a substantial redistribution of the elderly population.

International In-migration

The Census records persons entering Canada but does not record persons leaving Canada (only residents of Canada complete the census questionnaire; data on persons who have emigrated to another country are not available). While we do not know, therefore, how many elderly citizens have left Canada permanently, we do know that some 31,500 persons sixty-five and more years of age migrated from other countries to Canada during the 1976–1981 period (that is, over one in every hundred non-institutionalized elderly persons living in Canada in 1981 were recent immigrants). As observed for intraprovincial and interprovincial migration, international in-migration of persons fifty-five and older peaks at ages sixty-five to sixty-nine for older males and at ages sixty to sixty-four for older females and declines noticeably with increasing age. Again, females

TABLE 3.3

THE PERCENTAGES OF THE 1981 POPULATION WHO WERE MOVERS DURING 1976-81 BY SEX AND AGE, FOR CANADA

| Sex and Age (N) | Movers 1976-81 as a Percentage of the 1981 Population | | | | |
	Within the Same Municipality	Within the Same Province[1]	From a Different Province	From Outside Canada	Total[2]
Males					
55–59 (11,329)	14.9	8.0	2.0	1.2	26.2
60–64 (9,156)	14.2	7.9	2.1	1.5	25.7
65–69 (7,675)	13.9	9.0	2.1	1.7	26.8
70–74 (5,369)	14.0	7.1	1.8	1.3	24.1
75–79 (3,402)	12.9	6.3	1.5	1.2	21.9
80–84 (1,668)	13.4	6.9	1.3	0.7	22.2
85+ (965)	12.1	5.9	1.0	0.4*	19.5
Females					
55–59 (12,083)	15.8	7.5	2.1	1.5	27.0
60–64 (10,255)	15.6	8.7	2.2	1.9	28.5
65–69 (8,963)	16.7	8.1	2.0	1.7	28.4
70–74 (6,794)	16.3	7.5	1.8	1.6	27.1
75–79 (4,656)	15.8	6.6	1.6	1.5	25.5
80–84 (2,660)	15.9	6.7	1.8	1.2	25.7
85+ (1,515)	13.9	6.4	1.5	1.1	22.8

* The number of cases on which these data are based is less than ten. Estimates based on a small number of cases tend to be unreliable.

1. This category includes all who move across municipal boundaries within the same province.

2. Figures may not add to the total due to rounding errors.

SOURCE: The 1981 Public Use Sample Tape (2 percent sample), The 1981 Census of Canada.

appear to be more mobile than their male age peers (although these differences may be exaggerated by the relatively higher male risk of death, meaning that a greater percentage of male immigrants die and therefore are excluded from the census data while the female immigrants are more likely to survive to have their data recorded). One might speculate that a significant factor influencing the decision of older persons to migrate to Canada is the desire to follow non-elderly kin (for example, adult offspring) who have previously moved to Canada.

PATTERNS OF MOBILITY BY PROVINCE

Table 3.4 shows the mobility patterns of older males and females in each of the provinces and territories. This table indicates that older persons residing in the Atlantic Provinces (Newfoundland, Prince Edward Island, Nova Scotia, New Brunswick) are less likely to have moved in the past five years in comparison to older Canadians generally. More particularly, residents of the Atlantic Provinces are relatively unlikely to have moved locally or within the same province, and less likely to have come recently from another country. However, a larger than average percentage of the older residents of Prince Edward Island, Nova Scotia, and New Brunswick (but not Newfoundland) have moved recently from other Canadian provinces.[3]

Quebec and Ontario, because of their sizeable populations, largely account for the Canadian "average." Quebec, nevertheless, deviates noticeably with respect to the interprovincial and international in-migration of older persons. That is, a relatively small percentage of Quebec's older citizens have moved to Quebec from other provinces or from other countries. Quebec clearly is not a major retirement destination, as is southern Ontario or British Columbia.[4]

It is customary to discuss the Prairie Provinces of Manitoba, Saskatchewan and Alberta as a unit. Nevertheless, while Manitoba and Saskatchewan appear to have fairly "typical" patterns of older person mobility, Alberta is clearly the more important destination for older international in-migrants and particularly for in-migrants from other Canadian provinces. Alberta's "attraction" for non-Alberta residents may be explained in terms of Alberta's healthier, indeed, booming economy (during 1976–81) and by its proximity to the mountains. Further, older in-migrants to Alberta may be following adult offspring who have moved previously to Alberta to seek employment or, alternatively, may be expatriates returning home. As will be shown later, for example, there are significant flows of older migrants between Alberta and British Columbia. While the dominant flow is from Alberta to British Columbia, there is a significant counterflow from British Columbia to Alberta. Presumably, some of these older migrants moving from British Columbia to Alberta are ex-Albertans returning to their home province.

Table 3.4

The Percentages of the 1981 Population Who Were Movers During 1976–81 by Age and Sex, for Canada, the Provinces and the Territories

Province and Age	Within the Same Municipality		From the Same Province[1]		From a Different Province		From Outside Canada		Total[2]	
	M	F	M	F	M	F	M	F	M	F
Canada										
55–64	14.6	15.7	8.0	8.1	2.1	2.2	1.4	1.7	26.0	27.7
65–74	13.9	16.5	8.2	7.8	2.0	1.9	1.5	1.6	25.7	27.9
75+	12.9	15.5	6.4	6.6	1.3	1.6	0.9	1.3	21.6	25.1
Newfoundland										
55–64	7.8	9.2	4.3	4.5	1.1*	1.2*	—	0.5*	13.1	15.3
65–74	9.7	7.7	5.0	6.0	—	—	—	—	14.7	13.7
75+	7.6*	3.8	2.9*	2.0*	—	0.7*	—	0.7*	10.5	17.1
Prince Edward Island[3]										
55–64	9.0	8.6	3.3	4.9	4.3	5.9	0.7	0.5	17.3	20.1
65+	8.1	12.2	5.6	5.7	2.9	2.3	0.9	0.8	17.5	21.0
Nova Scotia										
55–64	10.0	11.0	4.2	4.2	2.7	3.2	0.4*	0.9*	17.4	19.2
65–74	10.8	14.6	4.9	3.6	3.0	2.1	0.8*	1.6*	19.6	21.9
75+	6.4	11.5	5.6	7.3	0.4*	1.0*	0.4*	2.0*	12.7	21.7
New Brunswick										
55–64	10.3	11.4	5.6	4.3	2.8	4.7	0.9*	0.8*	19.5	21.2
65–74	9.4	10.9	2.8	4.1	3.0	2.4	1.0*	0.7*	16.2	18.0
75+	9.7	10.9	5.1	4.1	1.0*	3.4*	—	0.7*	15.8	19.1

Movers 1976–81 as a Percentage of the 1981 Population

(Continued on the next page)

TABLE 3.4 (Continued)

Province and Age	Movers 1976–81 as a Percentage of the 1981 Population									
	Within the Same Municipality		From the Same Province[1]		From a Different Province		From Outside Canada		Total[2]	
	M	F	M	F	M	F	M	F	M	F
Quebec										
55–64	15.7	18.1	8.4	8.5	0.4	0.4	0.8	1.0	25.2	28.0
65–74	16.1	18.6	8.8	9.1	0.2*	0.5	0.9	1.0	25.9	29.3
75+	15.9	17.5	6.9	7.7	0.5*	0.3*	0.7*	0.8	23.9	26.3
Ontario										
55–64	14.4	14.9	8.2	8.3	1.3	1.5	1.5	1.9	25.4	26.6
65–74	13.7	16.4	7.9	8.3	1.4	1.5	1.9	2.4	24.9	28.4
75+	11.3	14.7	6.6	6.7	1.2	1.6	1.5	1.5	20.6	24.4
Manitoba										
55–64	15.5	16.6	5.3	5.9	1.6	1.7	1.1	2.0	23.5	26.1
65–74	14.0	16.4	6.2	4.0	2.2	1.3	0.5*	1.6	22.8	23.3
75+	16.9	17.4	4.4	2.3	0.8*	1.5*	0.3*	0.6*	22.5	21.8
Saskatchewan										
55–64	14.0	12.9	5.4	7.3	2.4	1.8	0.5*	0.6*	22.2	22.4
65–74	10.3	15.8	7.6	6.8	2.0	2.5	0.3*	—	20.2	25.1
75+	7.8	15.5	7.8	7.8	0.8*	0.7*	—	0.2*	16.4	24.3
Alberta										
55–64	15.9	17.1	6.1	7.6	4.7	5.1	2.0	2.5	28.7	32.3
65–74	15.5	17.2	6.4	5.6	3.2	4.2	2.5	1.4	27.6	28.5
75+	13.4	16.6	5.4	4.5	2.2	6.0	0.7*	2.0	21.7	29.1
British Columbia										
55–64	15.0	16.5	12.1	11.0	6.2	5.8	3.0	3.0	36.4	36.2
65–74	14.1	15.8	12.6	9.4	6.1	4.6	3.0	2.1	35.8	32.0
75+	15.9	15.6	7.3	8.0	3.7	2.6	1.0*	2.2	27.8	28.4

Yukon[3]										
55–64	20.4	20.8	3.6	5.0	11.7	12.9	1.5	2.0	37.2	39.6
65+	26.4	18.3	10.4	11.7	6.5	20.0	—	—	41.6	50.0
Northwest Territories[3]										
55–64	29.1	29.1	5.9	5.4	8.9	9.5	1.0	2.0	44.8	45.3
65+	23.1	25.6	4.9	3.4	2.1	4.3	0.7	1.7	31.5	34.2

* The number of cases on which these data are based is less than ten. Estimates based on a small number of cases tend to be unreliable.

1. This category includes all who move across municipal boundaries within the same province.

2. Figures may not add to the total due to rounding errors.

3. The 2 percent Public Use Sample aggregates Prince Edward Island, The Yukon and the Northwest Territories for reasons of confidentiality. For these areas, the data reported are from the 20 percent sample as published by Statistics Canada.

Source: The 1981 Public Use Sample Tape (2 percent sample), The 1981 Census of Canada; and Statistics Canada, The 1981 Census of Canada, Volume I, Catalogue Number 92–907, Table 1 (20 percent sample).

While the flows of older persons into Alberta are relatively high, there are even greater flows into British Columbia. This province enjoys a reputation as Canada's premier retirement location, and the migration flows of older persons into British Columbia (some 27,500 persons fifty-five and older in 1976–81) validate that reputation. Further, older British Columbians are somewhat more likely than the older residents of other provinces to move from one part of that province to another. In short, in no other province is the older population as likely to have been recently mobile.

The territories of the North are qualitatively different from the southern provinces. For example, the older populations of the Yukon and Northwest Territories are relatively small and highly mobile. They are far more likely than southern, older populations to move locally and to migrate in from other parts of Canada.

Finally, the mobility patterns of older males in comparison with older females are rather similar within any given province. Further, the mobility patterns of the various age groups in Tables 3.2 and 3.3 — 55–64, 65–74, and 75+ — are rather similar within any given province. There are, however, differences from one province to another, with mobility tending to be low in the East (Atlantic Provinces and Quebec) but high in the West (British Columbia, Alberta, and the Territories).

PATTERNS OF MOBILITY BY CENSUS METROPOLITAN AREA

Canada's larger cities and their immediate environs have been designated Census Metropolitan Areas (CMA's). In 1981, more than half of Canada's older population lived in these larger cities (56 percent of males fifty-five to sixty-four and 50 percent of males sixty-five and older; 57 percent of females fifty-five to sixty-four and sixty-five and older).

Table 3.5 shows the mobility patterns of older males and females in each of Canada's twenty-four largest cities. The data indicate that the mobility patterns of older males and females in any given city are very similar. Nevertheless, mobility patterns vary considerably from one city to another.

Cities in which approximately 30 percent or more of the older population have moved at least once in the past five years include Calgary, Edmonton, Montreal, Vancouver and Victoria. At the other end of the spectrum, cities in which approximately 24 percent or less of older residents have moved at least once in the past five years include Chicoutimi-Jonquière, St. Catharines-Niagara, St. John's (Nfld.), Sudbury, Thunder Bay and Windsor.

Turning to moves of a local nature, Montreal's older residents are more likely than the older residents of any other city to move locally.[5] Indeed, over 26 percent of male and over 29 percent of female Montrealers sixty-five and more years of aged moved locally at least once in the period 1976–81.

TABLE 3.5

THE PERCENTAGES OF THE 1981 POPULATION WHO WERE MOVERS DURING 1976–81 BY AGE AND SEX, FOR CANADA'S CENSUS METROPOLITAN AREAS (CMAs)

CMA and Age	Movers 1976–81 as a Percentage of the 1981 Population										Total[1]	
	Within the Same CMA		From the Same Province		From a Different Province		From Outside Canada					
	M	F	M	F	M	F	M	F			M	F
Calgary												
55–64	20.3	20.7	2.5	2.3	7.8	7.1	3.4	4.1			34.1	34.2
65+	20.2	22.2	2.3	2.5	4.6	5.5	3.4	3.1			30.5	33.2
Chicoutimi-Jonquière												
55–64	13.8	16.4	1.4	1.8	0.2	0.1	—	—			15.4	18.3
65+	19.7	21.2	3.0	3.1	—	—	—	0.2			22.4	24.7
Edmonton												
55–64	20.3	18.9	2.5	2.4	4.2	3.6	3.2	3.6			30.1	28.6
65+	19.5	23.6	3.0	2.8	2.8	4.0	2.0	2.4			27.3	32.9
Halifax												
55–64	19.7	18.7	2.2	1.8	3.0	3.2	0.6	1.0			25.5	24.7
65+	16.5	19.6	2.7	3.3	3.5	2.6	0.8	0.8			22.0	26.3
Hamilton												
55–64	16.6	18.9	3.0	3.2	1.0	1.2	0.9	1.4			21.5	24.7
65+	18.0	19.9	3.5	3.7	1.3	1.5	1.2	1.6			24.0	26.7
Kitchener												
55–64	18.3	17.0	4.8	6.1	1.5	1.6	1.2	2.1			25.8	26.7
65+	15.9	19.7	5.2	4.9	1.2	1.4	1.7	1.6			24.0	27.6

(Continued on the next page)

TABLE 3.5 (Continued)

CMA and Age	Within the Same CMA		From the Same Province		From a Different Province		From Outside Canada		Total[1]	
	M	F	M	F	M	F	M	F	M	F
London										
55–64	18.5	20.0	6.3	6.3	1.0	1.6	0.9	1.4	26.6	29.2
65+	20.6	19.9	6.9	6.2	1.6	1.4	1.1	1.6	30.1	29.1
Montreal										
55–64	26.6	28.3	1.5	1.6	0.5	0.4	1.3	1.8	29.8	32.0
65+	26.5	29.2	1.9	2.1	0.4	0.4	1.5	1.5	30.2	33.3
Oshawa										
55–64	15.6	17.5	7.8	8.7	1.4	1.5	0.6	1.2	25.5	28.8
65+	17.1	20.8	8.7	8.7	1.4	1.5	1.2	1.3	28.4	32.3
Ottawa-Hull (Ontario part)										
55–64	21.8	22.5	1.9	2.3	3.3	3.7	1.8	2.2	28.8	30.7
65+	19.3	20.6	2.1	2.8	4.1	4.4	1.5	1.4	27.0	29.3
Ottawa-Hull (Quebec part)										
55–64	19.7	23.6	2.7	3.4	0.8	0.3	0.7	0.6	23.8	27.9
65+	21.5	24.0	4.2	3.8	1.3	0.6	0.8	0.6	27.8	29.1
Quebec										
55–64	20.6	22.7	2.5	3.5	0.2	0.2	0.3	0.4	23.6	26.7
65+	22.9	25.9	3.0	3.1	0.2	0.3	0.3	0.3	26.6	29.5
Regina										
55–64	16.4	17.3	5.1	4.7	1.5	2.1	0.5	1.3	23.5	25.3
65+	16.8	21.6	4.7	3.3	1.2	2.3	0.8	1.1	23.5	28.3

Movers 1976–81 as a Percentage of the 1981 Population

	55-64 / 65+									
Saint John										
55–64	19.4	21.3	1.0	1.6	2.2	2.5	0.8	0.8	23.3	26.3
65+	19.8	22.5	1.1	1.9	1.5	2.3	0.8	0.8	23.1	27.4
Saskatoon										
55–64	15.9	16.7	5.4	4.7	4.8	3.7	0.7	1.8	26.7	26.9
65+	15.4	19.5	5.0	6.5	2.0	2.7	0.8	0.8	23.2	29.5
St. Catharines-Niagara										
55–64	15.0	17.4	4.0	4.3	1.4	1.4	0.8	1.2	21.2	24.2
65+	14.8	17.8	4.3	4.2	1.6	1.4	1.0	1.4	21.7	24.8
St. John's										
55–64	13.1	15.6	2.5	3.4	1.7	1.9	0.4	0.6	17.8	21.5
65+	16.0	16.2	2.4	3.4	0.7	0.8	0.1	0.4	19.1	20.8
Sudbury										
55–64	14.9	16.8	2.9	3.5	0.3	0.6	0.2	0.2	18.2	21.3
65+	18.2	18.2	3.4	4.5	0.3	0.6	0.1	0.7	22.1	24.0
Thunder Bay										
55–64	15.6	16.7	2.6	2.8	1.0	0.9	0.3	0.3	19.4	20.9
65+	17.1	20.0	2.7	2.1	0.4	0.9	0.4	0.4	20.4	23.3
Toronto										
55–64	21.0	21.9	1.6	1.9	1.6	1.7	3.3	4.5	27.6	30.1
65+	20.0	21.4	2.1	2.2	1.4	1.7	3.4	3.3	26.9	28.7
Trois-Rivières										
55–64	19.0	23.0	4.4	4.8	0.2	0.1	0.1	0.2	23.7	28.1
65+	21.9	24.2	6.3	6.3	0.1	0.2	0.3	0.3	28.6	31.0
Vancouver										
55–64	24.3	24.5	2.1	2.5	3.6	3.6	3.8	4.5	33.8	35.2
65+	21.8	22.8	2.5	2.3	3.2	3.1	3.3	3.2	30.7	31.4

(Continued on the next page)

TABLE 3.5 (*Continued*)

CMA and Age	Within the Same CMA		From the Same Province		From a Different Province		From Outside Canada		Total[1]	
	M	**F**	**M**	**F**	**M**	**F**	**M**	**F**	**M**	**F**
Victoria										
55–64	21.1	20.7	4.9	5.6	8.0	9.1	2.2	3.0	36.1	38.4
65+	20.0	21.6	4.8	4.2	8.3	6.0	2.3	1.9	35.3	33.6
Windsor										
55–64	18.1	18.6	2.0	2.0	0.5	0.4	1.4	1.7	21.9	22.6
65+	16.0	19.1	2.2	1.9	0.2	0.4	1.9	1.8	20.3	23.1
Winnipeg										
55–64	17.8	18.7	1.2	1.3	2.3	2.1	1.8	2.6	23.0	24.8
65+	18.6	20.8	1.7	1.4	1.7	1.9	1.4	1.6	23.3	25.6

1. Figures may not add to the total due to rounding errors.

SOURCE: Adapted from Statistics Canada, The 1981 Census of Canada, Volume I, Catalogue Number 92–907, Table 3 (20 percent sample).

Local moves outnumber moves involving longer distances. Cities in which approximately 5 percent or more of the elderly (sixty-five and older) population have come recently from elsewhere in the same province include Kitchener, London, Oshawa, Saskatoon and Trois-Rivières. With respect to the percentages of the elderly population that have moved recently from other provinces, the most notable cities are Victoria (with 7 percent of its residents sixty-five and more years of age recently having arrived from provinces other than British Columbia) and Calgary (at 5.1 percent). It is important to note that percentages and actual numbers can give quite different pictures. The actual number of in-migrants is discussed shortly.

Finally, cities in which over 3 percent of the elderly population have originated from outside of Canada during the past five years are Calgary, Toronto and Vancouver. Edmonton and Victoria are next, with over 2 percent of their elderly originating recently from outside Canada.

PATTERNS OF MOBILITY BY MOTHER TONGUE

(The reader may find the remaining presentation of data somewhat tedious and may want to skip to the summary at the end of this chapter — H.N.). Table 3.6 shows the five-year mobility patterns for all persons fifty-five and older in Canada in 1981 who claimed English, French, or some other language as their "mother tongue." The data show that the French are most likely to move locally and least likely to move interprovincially or to immigrate into Canada. Older persons whose mother tongue is neither English nor French are most likely to have immigrated to Canada. Indeed, over 4.5 percent of non-English, non-French fifty-five to sixty-four and also sixty-five to seventy-four, and about 2.5 percent of such persons seventy-five and older came to Canada in the 1976–81 period.

Because the bulk of the French Canadian population resides in Quebec, and because Ontario is adjacent to Quebec and of similar size, Table 3.6 examines the mobility patterns of the older French and English populations of Canada as a whole and for Quebec and Ontario, in particular. As noted for older French Canadians generally, the French in Quebec are more likely than the English in Quebec to move locally and less likely to have arrived recently from out-of-province. A similar pattern is evident in Ontario where the older French are again more likely than the English to move locally and less likely to have immigrated from another country. However, in Ontario, the older French are more likely than the English to have moved recently from another province (usually from Quebec).

PATTERNS OF MOBILITY BY SOCIO-ECONOMIC STATUS

Education and income are two commonly used measures of socio-economic status. Accordingly, Table 3.7 shows mobility patterns for older persons of

TABLE 3.6

THE PERCENTAGES OF THE 1981 POPULATION WHO WERE MOVERS DURING 1976–81 BY MOTHER TONGUE, AGE AND SEX, FOR CANADA, QUEBEC AND ONTARIO

Province, Mother Tongue, Age and Sex	(N)	Movers 1976-81 as a Percentage of the 1981 Population				
		Within the Same Municipality	From the Same Province[1]	From a Different Province	From Outside Canada	Total[2]
CANADA						
English						
55–64						
Male	(11,462)	14.1	8.3	2.6	0.9	26.0
Female	(12,734)	14.9	8.5	2.8	0.9	27.2
65–74						
Male	(7,505)	12.9	8.4	2.7	0.9	24.9
Female	(9,055)	15.4	7.7	2.3	1.0	26.4
75+						
Male	(3,383)	11.8	6.8	1.5	0.6	20.7
Female	(5,373)	14.9	6.7	1.8	1.1	24.5
French						
55–64						
Male	(4,898)	16.0	8.3	0.7	0.4	25.4
Female	(5,595)	18.1	8.3	0.9	0.4	27.6
65–74						
Male	(2,957)	16.0	8.6	0.6	0.6	25.8
Female	(3,808)	18.4	9.1	0.9	0.6	28.9
75+						
Male	(1,169)	16.0	6.9	0.3*	0.3*	23.5
Female	(1,770)	17.4	7.5	0.8	0.6	26.3
Other						
55–64						
Male	(4,125)	14.2	6.6	2.1	3.8	26.7
Female	(4,009)	14.9	6.5	1.9	5.9	29.2
65–74						
Male	(2,582)	14.6	7.2	1.6	4.4	27.8
Female	(2,894)	17.6	6.7	1.7	4.9	31.0
75+						
Male	(1,483)	12.9	5.3	1.8	2.2	22.1
Female	(1,688)	15.3	5.6	2.1	2.7	25.6
QUEBEC						
English						
55–64						
Male	(713)	13.6	9.3	1.4	1.3*	25.5
Female	(777)	16.6	8.2	0.9*	1.0*	26.8
65–74						
Male	(490)	14.9	7.8	0.4*	0.6*	23.7
Female	(586)	17.4	7.2	1.4*	0.3*	26.3
75+						
Male	(184)	14.1	8.2	1.1*	—	23.4
Female	(357)	15.7	7.8	0.3*	1.4*	25.2

(Continued on the next page)

TABLE 3.6 (*Continued*)

Province, Mother Tongue, Age and Sex	(N)	Within the Same Municipality	From the Same Province[1]	From a Different Province	From Outside Canada	Total[2]
French						
55–64						
Male	(4,067)	16.2	8.4	0.2*	0.4	25.2
Female	(4,644)	18.2	8.8	0.3	0.3	27.6
65–74						
Male	(2,404)	16.1	9.1	0.1*	0.6	25.9
Female	(3,188)	18.7	9.6	0.3	0.5	29.1
75+						
Male	(933)	16.7	7.1	0.3*	0.2*	24.3
Female	(1,441)	18.0	8.0	0.3*	0.4*	26.8
ONTARIO						
English						
55–64						
Male	(5,335)	14.2	8.7	1.3	0.8	25.1
Female	(5,986)	14.8	9.1	1.6	1.0	26.4
65–74						
Male	(3,356)	12.9	8.3	1.6	1.0	23.8
Female	(4,261)	15.5	8.8	1.5	1.2	27.0
75+						
Male	(1,547)	10.8	7.0	1.0	0.8	19.6
Female	(2,643)	14.6	7.2	1.2	0.9	24.0
French						
55–64						
Male	(427)	16.4	8.2	2.6	0.5	27.6
Female	(493)	20.1	5.3	2.0	0.4*	27.8
65+						
Male	(252)	20.6	6.0	1.6*	0.8*	29.0
Female	(308)	21.8	7.5	2.9*	0.3*	32.5
75+						
Male	(75)	16.2	8.1*	1.4*	—	25.7
Female	(154)	16.9	6.5	2.6*	1.3*	27.3

Movers 1976–81 as a Percentage of the 1981 Population (column header span)

* The number of cases on which these data are based is less than ten. Estimates based on a small number of cases tend to be unreliable.

1. This category includes all who move across municipal boundaries within the same province.

2. Figures may not add to the total due to rounding errors.

SOURCE: The 1981 Public Use Sample Tape (2 percent sample), The 1981 Census of Canada.

varying education, while Table 3.8 indicates the mobility of different income groups.

Table 3.7 reveals that those persons fifty-five years of age or older with a university education are most likely to move across a municipal boundary within the same province, are most likely to change their province of residence, and are most likely to have been a recent immigrant to Canada. While the university-educated group is the most mobile with respect to non-local moves, nevertheless, only a minority of Canada's older population has more than a high school education. The pattern is different for local moves in that those with less than a high school education are most likely to move shorter distances.

Turning now to total family income (or total personal income, for single persons), Table 3.8 indicates that the $30,000 income group of persons fifty-five years or older is least likely to move locally and tends to be more likely to move interprovincially. Indeed, the tendency to move locally seems to decrease with increasing income, especially for the fifty-five to sixty-four and sixty-five to seventy-four age groups.

TABLE 3.7

THE PERCENTAGES OF THE 1981 POPULATION WHO WERE MOVERS DURING 1976-81 BY EDUCATION, AGE AND SEX, FOR CANADA

		Movers 1976-81 as a Percentage of the 1981 Population				
Highest Level of Schooling, Age and Sex	(N)	Within the Same Muncipality	Within the Same Province[1]	From a Different Province	From Outside Canada	Total[2]
Less than Grade 9						
55-64						
Male	(7,558)	15.7	6.8	1.0	1.2	24.7
Female	(8,316)	17.3	7.2	1.3	1.9	27.7
65-74						
Male	(6,227)	14.5	7.0	1.2	1.4	24.0
Female	(7,267)	18.7	7.4	1.2	1.9	29.1
75+						
Male	(3,674)	12.7	6.0	0.9	0.7	20.4
Female	(4,898)	16.1	6.6	1.5	1.1	25.3
Grades 9-13[3]						
55-64						
Male	(7,308)	14.1	8.0	1.7	1.1	24.9
Female	(8,742)	15.0	8.4	2.3	1.5	27.2
65-74						
Male	(4,230)	13.6	9.0	2.3	1.3	26.1
Female	(5,338)	15.6	7.8	2.1	1.4	26.8
75+						
Male	(1,455)	13.7	6.2	1.8	0.7	22.4
Female	(2,552)	15.5	6.7	1.7	1.7	25.6
Other Non-University Education Only						
55-64						
Male	(2,909)	13.4	8.8	2.8	1.2	26.2
Female	(3,493)	14.9	8.7	3.3	1.4	28.3
65-74						
Male	(1,308)	13.1	10.6	3.7	1.9	29.4
Female	(2,065)	13.3	8.8	2.9	1.5	26.4
75+						
Male	(436)	12.2	8.3	1.8*	1.8*	24.1
Female	(935)	14.1	5.1	2.5	1.1	22.8

(Continued on the next page)

TABLE 3.7 *(Continued)*

Highest Level of Schooling, Age and Sex	(N)	Movers 1976-81 as a Percentage of the 1981 Population				
		Within the Same Muncipality	Within the Same Province[1]	From a Different Province	From Outside Canada	Total[2]
University[4]						
55-64						
Male	(2,710)	14.1	10.5	5.1	2.5	32.2
Female	(1,787)	13.3	9.6	3.5	2.2	28.7
65-74						
Male	(1,279)	13.2	8.6	3.6	3.0	28.5
Female	(1,087)	13.0	8.9	3.7	1.4	27.0
75+						
Male	(470)	12.1	8.7	2.8	2.1	25.7
Female	(446)	11.4	9.6	1.6*	1.8*	24.4

* The number of cases on which these data are based is less than ten. Estimates based on a small number of cases tend to be unreliable.

1. This category includes all who move across municipal boundaries within the same province.

2. Figures may not add to the total due to rounding errors.

3. Includes high school certificate, and trade certificate or diploma.

4. With or without certificate, diploma, or degree.

SOURCE: The 1981 Public Use Sample Tape (2 percent sample), The 1981 Census of Canada.

PATTERNS OF MOBILITY BY MARITAL STATUS

Table 3.9 shows that mobility patterns vary rather dramatically with marital status. In terms of total mobility, those older persons who are currently married are the least likely to move, while the separated and divorced are the most mobile (twice as likely to move as the currently married). The never married and the widowed are also more likely to be mobile than are the currently married, although these two groups are not as mobile as the separated and divorced.

This general pattern holds for local moves and for intraprovincial migration. The pattern of interprovincial migration is less clear; however, the separated and divorced, especially those sixty-five to seventy-four years of age, do tend to be the most mobile. There is also variation for international in-migrants. Never married elderly males appear to be very rare among the elderly recent arrivals to Canada. The marital status with the highest percentage of recent arrivals is the widowed (with the great majority of these being widows rather than widowers).

In summary, geographic mobility varies noticeably with marital status. The currently married, followed by the never married, are least likely to move. On the other hand, the separated and divorced, followed by the widowed, tend to be the most mobile.

TABLE 3.8

THE PERCENTAGES OF THE 1981 POPULATION WHO WERE MOVERS DURING 1976–81 BY INCOME, AGE AND SEX, FOR CANADA

| Income,[1] Age and Sex | (N) | Movers 1976–81 as a Percentage of the 1981 Population | | | | |
		Within the Same Municipality	Within the Same Province[2]	From a Different Province	From Outside Canada	Total[3]
Less than $10,000[4]						
55–64						
Male	(1,919)	14.0	10.6	2.2	3.2	30.5
Female	(2,905)	16.1	8.9	2.0	2.7	29.7
65–74						
Male	(2,558)	13.9	8.7	1.5	2.1	26.3
Female	(2,253)	13.9	7.5	1.3	1.5	24.1
75+						
Male	(1,549)	10.6	5.4	1.2	0.7	17.8
Female	(973)	11.3	4.9	0.8*	0.6*	17.8
$10,000–$19,999						
55–64						
Male	(3,940)	13.6	8.4	2.0	1.1	25.1
Female	(4,831)	14.0	8.0	2.0	1.2	25.2
65–74						
Male	(4,319)	12.4	8.2	2.2	0.9	23.7
Female	(3,591)	11.6	7.2	1.9	0.6	21.3
75+						
Male	(1,669)	10.9	5.3	1.1	0.5*	17.8
Female	(989)	9.7	4.7	1.0	0.9*	16.3
$20,000–$29,999						
55–64						
Male	(4,547)	11.9	6.8	1.8	0.7	21.2
Female	(4,113)	10.8	7.6	1.7	1.0	22.4
65–74						
Male	(1,853)	11.0	7.7	2.2	0.9	21.8
Female	(1,439)	10.8	7.6	2.0	0.8	21.3
75+						
Male	(419)	12.2	5.7	1.2*	1.2*	20.3
Female	(337)	9.8	4.7	0.6*	0.3*	15.4
$30,000+						
55–64						
Male	(6,814)	11.2	6.0	2.2	0.8	20.2
Female	(5,200)	11.1	5.9	2.2	0.7	19.9
65–74						
Male	(1,689)	9.5	5.6	1.8	1.2	18.1
Female	(1,259)	9.8	7.0	2.1	1.0	19.9
75+						
Male	(347)	8.8	6.1	1.3*	1.3*	17.6
Female	(286)	8.7	4.5	1.7*	0.7*	15.7

* The number of cases on which these data are based is less than ten. Estimates based on a small number of cases tend to be unreliable.

1. For families, income is total family income; for single persons, income is total personal income.
2. This category includes all who move across municipal boundaries within the same province.
3. Figures may not add to the total due to rounding errors.
4. Excludes those who reported a loss.

SOURCE: The 1981 Public Use Sample Tapes (2 percent sample), The 1981 Census of Canada.

NET MIGRATION OF THE ELDERLY
Net Interprovincial Migration

In Canada in 1976–81, some 45,000 (2.1 percent of) persons aged fifty-five to sixty-four and another 39,000 (1.8 percent of) persons aged sixty-five and older changed their province of residence. If these older interprovincial migrants originated from all parts of Canada but moved very specifically (for example, to southern Ontario or to British Columbia), then there might be some concern that such a migration pattern would, in time, become problematic. However, the interprovincial migration of older persons is not this selective. Table 3.10 shows the number of older persons leaving a given

TABLE 3.9

THE PERCENTAGES OF THE 1981 POPULATION WHO WERE MOVERS DURING 1976-81 BY MARITAL STATUS, AGE AND SEX, FOR CANADA

Marital Status, Age and Sex	(N)	Within the Same Municipality	Within the Same Province[1]	From a Different Province	From Outside Canada	Total[2]
Never Married						
55–64						
Male	(1,510)	22.5	8.5	1.4	0.7	33.2
Female	(1,442)	19.9	9.6	2.3	1.5	33.3
65–74						
Male	(944)	16.4	8.3	1.8	0.3*	26.8
Female	(1,330)	18.8	8.1	2.3	1.1	30.2
75+						
Male	(470)	14.0	8.5	1.1*	0.2*	23.8
Female	(872)	14.2	6.7	1.3	1.0*	23.2
Now Married						
55–64						
Male	(17,066)	12.2	7.4	2.1	1.4	23.1
Female	(15,776)	12.2	7.6	2.1	1.4	23.4
65–74						
Male	(10,457)	12.3	7.8	2.0	1.6	23.7
Female	(7,971)	11.5	7.4	1.8	1.2	21.9
75+						
Male	(4,023)	11.2	5.8	1.2	0.9	19.1
Female	(2,109)	10.8	5.5	1.1	0.9	18.3
Widowed						
55–64						
Male	(683)	20.2	9.5	1.2*	1.6	32.5
Female	(3,753)	22.4	8.6	2.1	3.0	36.0
65–74						
Male	(1,047)	20.2	9.3	2.0	2.0	33.5
Female	(5,863)	21.5	8.1	1.7	2.4	33.7
75+						
Male	(1,376)	15.8	7.3	1.7	1.2	26.0
Female	(5,693)	17.2	7.0	1.8	1.5	27.6

(Continued on the next page)

TABLE 3.9 (Continued)

Marital Status, Age and Sex	(N)	Movers 1976–81 as a Percentage of the 1981 Population				
		Within the Same Municipality	Within the Same Province[1]	From a Different Province	From Outside Canada	Total[2]
Divorced						
55–64						
Male	(624)	33.5	15.5	1.8	1.3*	52.1
Female	(791)	31.9	10.7	3.0	1.4	47.0
65–74						
Male	(265)	29.4	10.6	2.3*	1.1*	43.4
Female	(286)	30.4	9.1	4.2	0.7*	44.4
75+						
Male	(73)	34.2	9.6*	1.4*	—	45.2
Female	(79)	25.3	6.3*	1.3*	1.3*	34.2
Separated						
55–64						
Male	(602)	36.7	13.3	3.8	1.5*	55.3
Female	(576)	34.5	9.4	2.3	2.6	48.8
65–74						
Male	(331)	27.2	14.8	2.7*	1.5*	46.2
Female	(307)	27.4	12.1	3.3	1.3*	44.0
75+						
Male	(93)	21.5	8.6*	1.1*	1.1*	32.3
Female	(78)	20.5	10.3*	6.4*	1.3*	38.5

* The number of cases on which these data are based is less than ten. Estimates based on a small number of cases tend to be unreliable.

1. This category includes all who move across municipal boundaries within the same province.

2. Figures may not add to the total due to rounding errors.

SOURCE: The 1981 Public Use Sample Tape (2 percent sample), The 1981 Census of Canada.

TABLE 3.10

NET INTERPROVINCIAL MIGRATION IN CANADA 1976–81 BY AGE AND SEX

Province Age	Interprovincial Migration 1976–81							
	In-Migrants		Out-Migrants		Net Migration[1]		Net Migration Rate[2]	
	Male	Female	Male	Female	Male	Female	Male	Female
Canada[3]								
55–64	21,505	23,905	21,510	23,905	—	—	—	—
65+	16,950	22,335	16,955	22,335	—	—	—	—
Newfoundland								
55–64	225	285	320	330	−95	−45	−4.3	−2.2
65+	160	240	205	270	−45	−35	−1.7	−1.2
Prince Edward Island								
55–64	215	320	90	130	125	195	24.0	36.1
65+	180	175	75	115	100	60	11.7	6.1

(Continued on the next page)

TABLE 3.10 (Continued)

Province Age	In-Migrants Male	In-Migrants Female	Out-Migrants Male	Out-Migrants Female	Net Migration[1] Male	Net Migration[1] Female	Net Migration Rate[2] Male	Net Migration Rate[2] Female
Nova Scotia								
55–64	1,075	1,125	600	825	470	300	12.2	7.3
65+	725	945	420	690	300	255	5.6	4.1
New Brunswick								
55–64	870	880	565	635	305	245	10.2	7.8
65+	565	780	395	680	165	100	4.1	2.1
Quebec								
55–64	1,175	1,065	5,485	6,465	−4,310	−5,400	−15.0	−17.4
65+	775	1,030	4,830	6,970	−4,055	−5,940	−12.9	−14.8
Ontario								
55–64	5,385	6,395	5,330	5,645	50	745	0.1	1.7
65+	4,715	7,370	3,600	4,315	1,110	3,060	2.4	5.1
Manitoba								
55–64	945	1,025	1,680	1,830	−735	−805	−14.8	−15.0
65+	750	1,080	1,455	1,805	−710	−730	−10.1	−8.9
Saskatchewan								
55–64	955	1,135	1,345	1,620	−395	−485	−8.3	−10.1
65+	760	1,010	1,320	1,850	−560	−835	−7.9	−11.2
Alberta								
55–64	3,690	3,650	3,760	3,970	−70	−320	−0.9	−4.0
65+	2,110	3,170	2,750	2,895	−640	270	−6.7	2.6
British Columbia								
55–64	6,810	7,895	1,975	2,160	4,830	5,735	40.0	43.9
65+	6,175	6,460	1,700	2,610	4,485	3,850	27.7	20.4
Yukon								
55–64	80	65	150	115	−65	−50	−78.8	−77.5
65+	25	60	75	55	−50	10	−77.5	22.7
Northwest Territories								
55–64	90	70	205	185	−115	−115	−95.0	−119.8
65+	15	25	120	75	−105	−55	−106.1	−67.9

1. In-migrants minus out-migrants may not exactly equal net migration due to rounding.

2. The net migration rate for the 65+ year olds is calculated as the

$$\frac{\text{Net migration 1976–1981 for persons 65+ in 1981}}{\text{Total population 60+ in 1976}} \times 1,000$$

Similarly, the net migration rate for the 55–64 year olds is calculated as the

$$\frac{\text{Net migration 1976–1981 for persons 55–64 in 1981}}{\text{Total population 50–59 in 1976}} \times 1,000$$

The 1976 population figures are taken from Statistics Canada, The 1976 Census of Canada, Volume 2, Catalogue Number 92-823, Table II.

3. The figures for Canada indicate the number of persons who changed their province of residence between 1976 and 1981.

SOURCE: Statistics Canada, The 1981 Census of Canada, Volume I, Catalogue Number 92-907, Table I (20 percent sample).

province in 1976–81, the number coming to a given province, the net gain or loss, and the rate of gain or loss.

The flows of older interprovincial migrants clearly do not move in only one direction. That is, there are flows of older persons both leaving and entering any given province. Newfoundland, for example, experienced a loss of 1,125 persons fifty-five years of age and older but at the same time gained 910 older persons for a small net loss. Those provinces reporting the most discrepant flows of older persons are Quebec — which lost almost 24,000 while gaining only 4,000 for a net loss of 20,000, and British Columbia — which received over 27,000 while losing some 8,000 for a net gain of 19,000 older persons.

In absolute numbers, the province experiencing the greatest net loss of older persons is Quebec, followed by Manitoba and Saskatchewan. The province with the greatest net increase in older persons is British Columbia, followed by Ontario and then by the Maritime Provinces (Prince Edward Island, Nova Scotia, New Brunswick).

Turning to the net number of older persons gained or lost per 1,000 older residents, British Columbia and then Prince Edward Island show the greatest rates of gain. On the other side of the coin, the Northwest Territories and the Yukon, followed by Quebec, Manitoba and Saskatchewan, show the greatest rates of loss. The remaining provinces — Newfoundland, Nova Scotia, New Brunswick, Ontario and Alberta — all report rather modest rates of net migration.

The interprovincial flows of migrants aged sixty-five and over for 1976–81 are illustrated in Figure 3.1.[6] These data are taken from the 1981 Census (2 percent sample) and represent 39,200 elderly interprovincial migrants. Figure 3.1 shows that the general direction of elderly migration is westward. While there are eastward flows, nevertheless, these are not as strong as the westward streams. Indeed, of all interprovincial migrants aged sixty-five and older in 1976–81, 71 percent moved to a province west of their 1976 place of residence; only 29 percent moved east of their 1976 place of residence. (These data treat New Brunswick, Nova Scotia, and Prince Edward Island as a single unit and ignore the Territories.) In other words, an elderly person is almost two and a half times as likely to move westward as eastward.

These patterns of interprovincial migration indicate a process of minor population redistribution, with the elderly population gradually shifting westward to concentrate in Ontario and particularly in British Columbia. Figure 3.2 illustrates this process of population redistribution — by showing the net migration exchanges (net gains or net losses) of persons sixty-five and older between pairs of provinces for the 1976–81 period (net exchanges of less than 500 elderly persons are not shown). For three provinces — Quebec, Ontario, and British Columbia — the magnitude of the net migration flows are especially notable. Quebec has a relatively heavy net loss of

500 Migrants = →

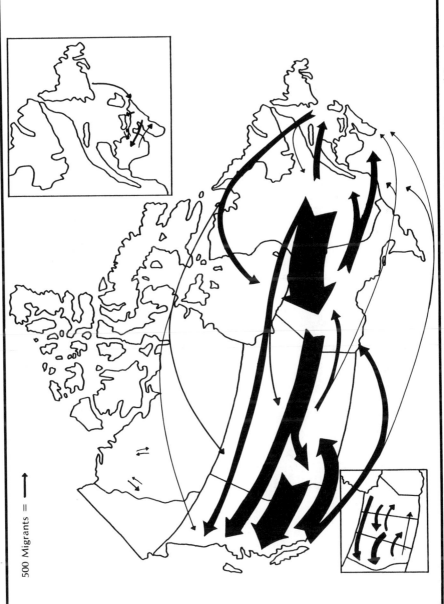

SOURCE: Based on data from the 1981 Public Use Sample Tape (2 percent sample), The 1981 Census of Canada.

FIGURE 3.2

NET INTERPROVINCIAL MIGRATION OF PERSONS AGED SIXTY-FIVE AND OLDER, 1976–81 (IN THOUSANDS)

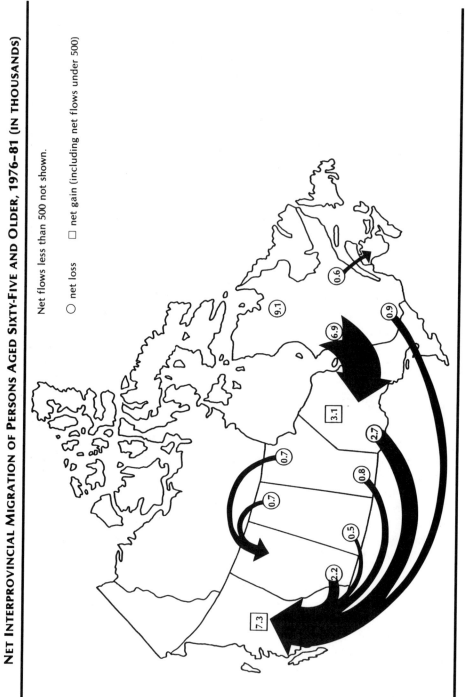

Net flows less than 500 not shown.

○ net loss □ net gain (including net flows under 500)

SOURCE: See Fig. 3.1; Format: Kosinski, 1976.

elderly persons (most going to Ontario). British Columbia and Ontario show the largest net gains, with Ontario's net increase coming almost entirely from Quebec, and British Columbia's largest net gains coming from Ontario, Alberta, Quebec, Manitoba, and Saskatchewan, in that order. It would appear that these interprovincial migration patterns do have a tendency to redistribute and to concentrate the elderly population in selected locations.

Net Migration by Mother Tongue

Given that the migration of older persons was heavier from Quebec than to Quebec during 1976–81, one might speculate about the effects of language on interprovincial migration. Table 3.11 shows the net interprovincial migration of older persons whose mother tongue is English or French (non-English and non-French are not reported in this table). With respect to the older Francophone population, Quebec experienced a modest net loss (1,180 persons) while the Maritimes (Prince Edward Island, Nova Scotia, New Brunswick), Alberta, and especially British Columbia experienced modest net gains. In Ontario, there was a net loss of older Francophone males, but an increase in older Francophone females.

While Quebec experienced a net loss of 1,180 older Francophones, in sharp contrast, Quebec had a net loss of almost 15,000 older Anglophones (more than fifty-five years of age). Remember that the French far out-number the English in Quebec and so these differentials in net migration are all the more striking. It would appear that this heavy out-flow of older Anglophones from Quebec during 1976–81 was a response, in part at least, to the politics of the Parti Quebecois which came to power in 1976 and sought, for example, independence in the form of "sovereignty-association" and made French the official language in Quebec. In the 1971–76 period pre-ceding the Parti Quebecois rise to power, 3,325 persons sixty-five and older came to Quebec from other provinces while 6,160 left Quebec for other provinces for a net loss of 2,835 (see the 1976 Census, publication no. 92-828, Table 36). In contrast, as noted earlier in Table 3.10, for 1976–81, fewer persons sixty-five and older came to Quebec (1,805 — down from the 1971–76 period's 3,325), and more left Quebec (11,800 — up from 6,160). From 1971–76 to 1976–81, Quebec's net loss increased over 3.5 times (to 9,995 — up from a net loss of 2,835). In short, during the 1976 to 1981 period, in-migration to Quebec declined and out-migration increased. As Table 3.11 shows, the great majority of these elderly out-migrants were Anglophones.

The Prairie Provinces also reported significant net losses of Anglophones fifty-five and older. The Maritimes, however, experienced modest net gains as did Ontario. Ontario had a relatively high net gain of females sixty-five years of age and older suggesting an in-flow of elderly widows. Of course,

Changing Residence

Table 3.11

Net Internal Migration 1976–81 by Mother Tongue,[1] Age and Sex, for Canada's Provinces

Province	English 55–64 Male	Female	65+ Male	Female	French 55–64 Male	Female	65+ Male	Female
Newfoundland	−70	−5	−40	−15	−15	−20	−10	−10
Prince Edward Island	110	165	80	65	10	30	15	5
Nova Scotia	440	260	305	260	70	55	15	−25
New Brunswick	240	115	115	10	70	120	60	95
Quebec	−3,320	−3,990	−3,080	−4,530	−130	−485	−135	−430
Ontario	−20	405	870	2,260	−165	5	−95	350
Manitoba	−555	−590	−640	−590	−5	−30	10	10
Saskatchewan	−280	−355	−390	−485	−15	30	−5	−35
Alberta	−120	−235	−440	85	40	10	10	55
British Columbia	3,725	4,345	3,335	2,960	160	305	155	−15
Yukon	−60	−40	−30	15	10	−5	−10	—
Northwest Territories	−80	−80	−90	−35	−20	−15	−10	−15

1. Persons whose mother tongue is neither English nor French are not reported in this table.
Source: Statistics Canada, The 1981 Census of Canada, Volume I, Catalogue Number 92–907, Table 9 (20 percent sample).

British Columbia also experienced striking net gains of Anglophones (over 14,000 persons).

An analysis of the 2 percent Public Use Sample regarding movement to and from the province of Quebec (data not shown) indicates that French-speaking older migrants who leave Quebec are most likely to move to either Ontario or New Brunswick. French-speaking older migrants who come to Quebec are most likely to arrive from Ontario. Those older persons migrating from Quebec who claim a mother tongue other than English or French are most likely to move to Ontario or British Columbia. Older non-English or non-French persons moving to Quebec tend to come from Ontario and are relatively rare. The non-English, non-French movement patterns resemble the Anglophone patterns more than the Francophone. English-speaking older persons are most likely to leave Quebec for Ontario or British Columbia; relatively few Anglophones — mostly from Ontario — move to Quebec.

Net Census Metropolitan Area Migration

Table 3.12 shows the numbers of older persons migrating to and from Canada's twenty-four largest cities.[7] This table also shows the net gain or loss of older persons through migration.

Canada's three largest cities — Montreal, Toronto, and Vancouver — experienced substantial flows of older persons both to and from each city. With respect to net migration, however, Montreal and Toronto both reported substantial net losses between 1976 and 1981 (Montreal had a net loss of 21,000 older persons while Toronto lost 10,000). Vancouver, on the other hand, reported only a small net loss of older persons. Given Vancouver's central location in Canada's Sunbelt, one might have expected a net gain of older migrants. It may be that Vancouver's high cost of living and its large urban character are less attractive to older persons than are the smaller cities and towns in British Columbia's southeastern coastal and south central interior areas.

Other cities with relatively heavy in-flows and out-flows of older persons are Ottawa, Hamilton, Winnipeg, Calgary, Edmonton, and Victoria. Of these, Edmonton and Winnipeg experienced the heaviest net losses (2,390 and 2,365), while Victoria experienced substantial net gains, with older in-migrants outnumbering older out-migrants by over 3,600 persons.

Overall, Canada's twenty-four larger cities experienced a net loss of over 34,000 older persons indicating that persons fifty-five years of age and older are more likely to move away from, rather than to, these larger metropolitan areas. These data, however, do not show the destinations of these out-migrants. Many may simply move to nearby towns and therefore remain within the orbit of these larger cities.

THE 1981 WINNIPEG AND EDMONTON AREA SURVEYS

In 1981, the Population Research Laboratory of the Department of Sociology at the University of Alberta and the Department of Sociology at the University of Manitoba conducted surveys on representative samples of the populations of Winnipeg and Edmonton. Included in these samples were one hundred persons fifty-five years of age or older living in Winnipeg and another eighty-six persons living in Edmonton. Of these, one-half in each city were sixty-five years of age or older. Winnipeg had proportionately more of the older elderly population (seventy-five or older) and consequently more females and more widows (because females outlive males). Winnipeg's older persons tended to be of somewhat higher socio-economic status (higher income and education) than Edmonton's older residents.

With respect to geographic mobility, 24 percent of older Winnipegers, but only 3 percent of older Edmontonians, had lived all of their lives in their respective cities. These data reflect the fact that Winnipeg is a long-established, older city, while Edmonton is a younger city having experi-

TABLE 3.12

NET CENSUS METROPOLITAN AREA MIGRATION IN CANADA 1976–81 BY AGE AND SEX[1]

| CMA and Age | Census Metropolitan Area Migration 1976–81 | | | | | |
| | In-Migrants | | Out-Migrants | | Net Migration[2] | |
	Male	Female	Male	Female	Male	Female
Calgary						
55–64	1,870	1,850	2,055	2,120	−185	−270
65+	935	1,505	1,455	1,715	−520	−210
Chicoutimi-Jonquière						
55–64	80	105	120	215	−40	−110
65+	100	130	155	200	−50	−70
Edmonton						
55–64	1,425	1,365	2,455	2,275	−1,030	−905
65+	980	1,520	1,390	1,560	−140	−45
Halifax						
55–64	540	580	720	895	−175	−310
65+	395	725	560	620	−170	100
Hamilton						
55–64	1,040	1,215	1,155	1,260	−115	−45
65+	1,050	1,575	905	1,235	145	340
Kitchener						
55–64	710	970	585	670	130	305
65+	630	870	425	515	210	360
London						
55–64	890	1,080	815	940	80	140
65+	895	1,175	655	890	245	290
Montreal						
55–64	2,295	2,755	7,905	9,120	−5,610	−6,365
65+	2,140	3,725	6,490	8,375	−4,350	−4,645
Oshawa						
55–64	535	605	455	425	80	180
65+	440	625	290	400	155	230
Ottawa-Hull (Ontario part)						
55–64	1,205	1,585	1,860	2,005	−655	−420
65+	1,050	1,995	995	1,200	55	795
Ottawa-Hull (Quebec part)						
55–64	205	225	200	240	—	−20
65+	210	225	125	140	90	90
Quebec						
55–64	575	960	815	1,040	−240	−80
65+	550	915	725	1,015	−180	−105
Regina						
55–64	410	490	580	635	−170	−150
65+	340	440	400	565	−65	−120
Saint John						
55–64	140	220	370	385	−225	−165
65+	110	280	230	315	−115	−40

(Continued on the next page)

TABLE 3.12 (*Continued*)

CMA and Age	Census Metropolitan Area Migration 1976–81					
	In-Migrants		Out-Migrants		Net Migration[2]	
	Male	Female	Male	Female	Male	Female
Saskatoon						
55–64	550	530	475	585	85	−60
65+	385	710	430	590	−40	125
St. Catharines-Niagara						
55–64	835	985	520	655	320	330
65+	830	1,030	465	700	370	325
St. John's						
55–64	225	295	235	295	−5	5
65+	145	285	175	245	−30	35
Sudbury						
55–64	200	270	525	470	−325	−195
65+	175	270	275	320	−100	−55
Thunder Bay						
55–64	210	240	345	340	−130	−105
65+	165	195	255	260	−95	−65
Toronto						
55–64	4,170	5,110	7,410	8,570	−3,235	−3,460
65+	3,535	5,960	6,040	7,000	−2,510	−1,045
Trois-Rivières						
55–64	205	270	185	220	20	45
65+	245	380	165	275	80	105
Vancouver						
55–64	3,215	4,005	3,955	4,195	−735	−190
65+	3,205	4,105	3,500	3,525	−290	575
Victoria						
55–64	1,550	2,165	1,000	1,145	555	1,020
65+	1,975	2,200	860	1,275	1,120	920
Windsor						
55–64	270	300	590	600	−320	−300
65+	250	335	450	530	−200	−195
Winnipeg						
55–64	910	1,060	1,620	1,780	−710	−720
65+	890	1,215	1,315	1,720	−425	−510

1. International in-migrants and out-migrants are not included in this table.
2. Figures may not add exactly due to rounding errors.
SOURCE: Statistics Canada, The 1981 Census of Canada, Volume 1, Catalogue Number 92–907, Table 3 (20 percent sample).

enced a great deal of growth since the oil boom following World War II. Just the same, 47 percent of older Edmontonians were born in Alberta and 64 percent grew up in Alberta. In comparison, 61 percent of older Winnipegers were born in Manitoba (including the 24 percent born in Winnipeg) and 70 percent grew up in that province. In short, both cities have experienced considerable in-migration from within their respective provinces.

This pattern reflects the rural-urban migration that played such a dramatic role during the first half of the twentieth century and accompanied the shift from rural, agricultural economies to urban-based industrial and service economies. Concerning those persons born out-of-province, most originated in Europe (about one-quarter of both older Edmontonians and Winnipegers) or in Saskatchewan (13 percent of Edmontonians and 6 percent of Winnipegers).

Finally, these older residents were asked if they had plans to move. Only 2 percent in each city had plans to move away from the city, while another 3 percent in Edmonton and 6 percent in Winnipeg had plans to move within the city. While these data present a picture of residential stability, nevertheless, persons who have previously left Winnipeg or Edmonton for other destinations are not included in the samples. A survey of the older residents of Victoria, Vancouver, or Penticton would find many who have arrived relatively recently from out-of-province, including, perhaps, arrivals from Edmonton and Winnipeg.

SUMMARY

In summary, while older persons are less likely to move than are the non-elderly, nevertheless, Canada's older citizens do exhibit substantial rates of geographic mobility (approximately one in four older persons moved in the five-year period from 1976 to 1981). Most moves are local in nature, although there are significant movements across municipal, provincial and even national boundaries. Older movers are somewhat more likely to be recently retired, to be separated, divorced or widowed rather than married, and to be female rather than male. Higher levels of income and education predict higher levels of interprovincial moves; lower income and lower education groups (and females) are more likely to move locally. Francophones are more likely to move locally than are Anglophones and are least likely to move interprovincially. There are also significant regional differences in the propensity to move, with mobility being relatively low in the Atlantic region and in Quebec but relatively high in the Prairies and in British Columbia. Interprovincial migration tends to be westward in direction rather than eastward, and the more popular provincial destinations are British Columbia, Alberta, and southern Ontario. There is evidence that for the 1976 to 1981 period, there was a significant exodus of older Anglophones from Quebec, with the majority of these persons going to Ontario. In terms of net migration, there is evidence that the older population is being somewhat redistributed geographically. Places experiencing net losses of older residents include Quebec, the Prairies, and many of the larger cities across Canada (the CMA's). Places experiencing net gains of older persons include British Columbia, southern Ontario and selected cities such as Victoria and St. Catharines-Niagara.

NOTES

1. Many elderly persons who leave Canada for less than six months at a time simply have their mail forwarded from their Canadian address. In other words, these seasonal migrants do not register a change of address with the Old Age Security mailing office. Therefore, the OAS data underestimate the number of OAS recipients who are out of the country at any given time and underestimate the number of OAS cheques spent outside of Canada.

2. It might be expected that mobility rates will rise slightly for the older elderly as the likelihood of a move (or a series of moves) into an institutional setting increases. This anticipated upturn in mobility rates towards the end of life is not evident in the data. Recall, however, that the census data exclude the institutionalized population, and therefore moves into institutional settings are excluded. It follows, therefore, that census data likely underestimate the probability of mobility near the end of the life span.

3. Note that at this point we are examining the mobility status of persons who lived in a given province in 1981. These data do not record those who have moved away from a given province. Therefore, the picture of mobility for New Brunswick, for example, excludes ex-New Brunswickers. Migration to and from given provinces is examined shortly.

4. As a note of interest, the in-migration of older persons to Quebec from other countries, although relatively rare, is some two times as frequent as the in-migration of older persons from other Canadian provinces. The effect of mother tongue on migration will be examined in greater detail shortly.

5. As will be shown shortly, the Francophone population is more likely to move locally than is the Anglophone population. This pattern may reflect observations that there is relatively little migration into Quebec, and that the resident Francophone population tends to stay in Quebec. Relocations of the older Francophone population tend to be shorter-distance moves within the local area rather than longer-distance migration.

6. Figure 3.1 illustrates the migration flows of elderly persons (sixty-five and older) between Canada's regions (the Atlantic Provinces, Quebec, Ontario, the Prairie Provinces, British Columbia, and the North). Two inserts on Figure 3.1 show the migration flows between the three Prairie Provinces and between the four Atlantic Provinces. This analysis was also done for the older (fifty-five and older) population (data not shown). The pattern of interprovincial migration for Canadians aged fifty-five and older is very similar to the pattern for the population sixty-five years of age and older.

7. In this discussion, "migrants" include both interprovincial and intraprovincial migrants. International migrants are excluded.

CHAPTER 4

MOBILITY AND THE LIFE SPAN

It is well known that the likelihood of a person changing his or her residence depends, in part, on that person's age. This chapter explores mobility across the life span by means of a review of relevant literature and a presentation of data from the 1981 Census (2 percent sample). These data will indicate the probabilities of persons of various ages changing their places of residence. Actually, while such a cross-sectional picture (data across persons of various ages) appears to suggest a pattern of moves across the life span, these data may be misleading. If there is no change from one generation to another, then the cross-sectional picture does reveal the pattern of moves across the life span. However, if one generation is more or less likely to move than another, then the cross-sectional picture confounds the age and generation (cohort) effects. Ideally, one would follow successive generations across their life spans in order to separate the age and cohort effects, but such a study done prospectively would take a researcher more than one lifetime. A retrospective study would be more efficient, providing that good data could be obtained. Inasmuch as the census mobility data go back as far as 1961, various cohorts can be examined retrospectively to that date.

Following a review of the literature, this chapter examines the 1981 cross-sectional data to indicate the probabilities of various kinds of moves for each age cohort. Finally, this chapter compares the mobility patterns of the 1981, 1976, 1971, and 1961 cohorts of elderly Canadians.

MOBILITY ACROSS THE LIFE SPAN: A REVIEW OF THE LITERATURE

It is, by now, a truism that the propensity to change one's residence varies with age. Generally, age is taken as an indicator of a person's position in the life cycle. Young adults have the highest rates of mobility because it is in young adulthood that one leaves home to live on one's own, goes off to college, finds permanent employment, finds a mate, purchases a home, and/or begins to have children. Young adulthood, then, implies all these various life cycle transitions and their accompanying residential moves. In middle age, mobility rates decline as careers solidify and as families settle into home, school, and community life. (The mobility patterns of children reflect the patterns of their parents and also influence those patterns, for example, the presence of school-age children tends to constrain parental mobility.) Nevertheless, life cycle events and transitions continue to influence the tendency to move. Factors such as increased income coupled with a desire for a better or larger home, divorce, job transfer, unemployment, retirement, or death of a spouse tend to increase the propensity to move. For example, Henretta (1986) found that elderly retirees are more likely to move than are non-retirees.

Liaw and Nagnur (1985) fitted Canadian migration data to a mathematical model (the Rogers-Castro model) that reflects the age-related pattern of mobility described in the paragraph above. The Rogers-Castro model assumes that mobility declines from birth until the teens when it rises rapidly to a peak in the mid-twenties. From this peak, mobility declines rapidly until middle age and then continues to decline, although more slowly, with increasing age. In addition, the model predicts a modest increase in mobility rates around the age of retirement.

Liaw and Nagnur (1985) examined migration from Canada's non-metropolitan areas and from the twenty-three largest cities (Census Metropolitan Areas) for the 1971-76 period. They note that females are more mobile over short distances than are males, and that the peak in female mobility rates comes at an earlier age (about two years earlier) than for males. Further, the female mobility rate rises faster and falls faster than does the male curve. Liaw and Nagnur also note a small peak about the age of retirement for both males and females. This retirement peak comes about three years of age earlier for females than males, reflecting, for the most part, the age difference between spouses.

Liaw and Nagnur (1985, 92-94, 99) find that migration from non-metropolitan to metropolitan areas is relatively low for families with young dependents, is slightly higher for females than males, and shows a relatively weak retirement peak. In contrast, the metropolitan centres of Montreal and Toronto show rather substantial retirement out-migration peaks, although Vancouver, a retirement centre, does not. Indeed, many of the Canadian CMAs fail to show a retirement out-migration peak, and there is considerable variation in the peak age for those which do. Finally, in most CMAs, the mobility of elderly females exceeds that of elderly males.

Migration is, of course, not simply a function of age. At any point in time, and at any age, variables such as socio-economic status, ethnicity, gender, marital status, employment status, family status, and so on, all play a role in the decision to migrate or not. Age, nevertheless, is a key variable and, because it overlaps with important cohort and period variables, it is important to examine the effects of age, cohort, and period separately.

Age implies not only biological age but also, as argued above, position in the life cycle. Retirement migration and moves in later life occasioned by declining health are examples of age-related migration. Period effects are quite different; they refer to specific events or short-term conditions that influence current migration patterns. For example, the recession in the early 1980s, the Parti Quebecois–Levesque era in the province of Quebec, or the oil boom and bust in Alberta, may have temporarily distorted or affected longstanding migration patterns.

In contrast to the age and period variables, a cohort is a group of people born about the same time, who tend to have had similar life experiences. This similarity in history and experience may predict migration independently of the age and period variables. For example, it is often argued that recent cohorts of older persons are more likely to engage in long-distance retirement migration and may choose somewhat different destinations than earlier cohorts (see, for example, Frey 1986). Recent cohorts of older persons, more so than earlier groups, have travelled on vacation and business and have been more likely to move for employment reasons. This mobility has become, early in life, a part of these cohorts' life-styles and suggests that successive groups of elderly persons will be increasingly mobile. Such a shift in behaviour across successive generations is an example of a cohort effect.

In short, migration is significantly influenced by age, cohort, and period factors, each of which tends to have independent effects on the propensity to move. For example, Pitcher et al. (1985) found that age, period, and cohort had independent effects on the migration of American males in the 1966–76 period. More specifically, they found, for retirement-aged white men, although not for blacks of the same age, an increase in the propensity to migrate. This age-related retirement peak was independent of the cohort and period effects. The cohort analysis suggested that whites (but not blacks) in the United States were increasingly likely to migrate, even though the period analysis showed a slight decline in migration propensity (Pitcher et al. 1985, 112). It is likely that the separate effects of the age, cohort, and period variables observed in the United States would also be observable in Canada. Further, just as these variables have different effects on blacks and whites in the United States, it is likely that they will have different effects on various groups in Canada. For example, as shown in Chapter 3, the effect of the Parti Quebecois period on the out-migration of older Anglophones from Quebec was substantially different from that period's effect on Francophone out-migration.

Frey (1984), in his examination of migration within six large American cities (Standard Metropolitan Statistical Areas), also notes the importance of age, period, and cohort effects. Frey (1984, 805) states that in the 1950–70 period, young adult whites in the early stages (that is, prechild and child-rearing stages) of the traditional family cycle (age effect) tended to be drawn to the central city. However, these moves tended to be temporary, and as the family reached the childrearing stage, there emerged a clear preference for the suburbs. The great majority of these moves occurred in early adulthood. While blacks were also most likely to move in early adult-hood, discrimination in white-dominated neighbourhoods (period effect) prevented their move to the suburbs. Frey observes that times are changing in that whites in 1970–80 are less likely (cohort effect) to enter into the tradi-tional family pattern, that is, there are more childless couples, more dual-earner families, and more single persons (never married, divorced). Consequently, there has recently emerged a modest movement of whites into the central cities. On the other hand, social change in the area of improved race relations (Frey 1984, 806) and improved economic oppor-tunity have meant that, recently, blacks have been more likely to move to the suburbs. Age still remains a key determinant of migration; however, social change is clearly evident in the evolving cohort patterns. Frey argues (1984, 804), however, that a redistribution of population comes slowly because most movement is confined to the younger age groups, while the middle aged and elderly tend to be immobile. Recent cohort changes then have little immediate effect on the overall distribution of the population. In the long term, of course, these effects can be substantial and may greatly reduce disparities in the social composition of central city and suburban areas.

"Gentrification" (McPherson 1983, 288) is another process that illustrates cohort change. Older generations have had a preference for suburban liv-ing. Recent generations, especially the younger, highly educated profes-sionals, increasingly seek to live in the inner city so as to be near the central business district. As a consequence, rent and property values in the inner city have tended to rise. Further, there is a tendency for certain groups, such as the elderly, to be displaced and forced to move elsewhere.

The literature reviewed above suggests that migration is related to age/stage in the lifecourse and that there are substantial variations from young adulthood to middle age and to old age in the tendency to change residential location. Cribier (1980, 256) notes that, among the elderly them-selves, the tendency to move is related to age and to position in the life cycle. For example, Cribier observes that in France the retired elderly are more likely to move than persons of the same age who remain employed. Further, among the elderly, mobility tends to decrease with increasing age. Among the retired, the recently retired, who tend to be the younger elderly, are most likely to move. Cribier (1980, 257–59; see also 1975, 363) describes five types of aged residential mobility (also reviewed previously in Chapter 2). First of all, employed persons nearing the end of their working career occasionally seek a transfer to, or seek new work in a location in which they desire to retire. Such preretirement mobility is rare in France and England (and in Canada?), but may be more common in the United States. Cribier's second, and more important form of elderly migration, is the movement of the recently retired shortly following withdrawal from the labour force. This retirement migration may be motivated by a desire to improve one's life-style, may be return migration (return to region of birth), or may constitute a move to be near or to live with kin. Cribier's third form of elderly migration typically involves the frail elderly, that is, the very old (and the prematurely disadvantaged) who are often female and who are forced to move due to declining health and/or loss of income (perhaps occasioned by death of a pensioned spouse or simply by the erosion of life savings). Moves for the frail elderly often involve institutionalization. Cribier discusses a fourth form of elderly migration which she suggests is related to neither biological age nor to the lifecourse, per se. This mobility is generally local in nature, involving short-distance moves motivated by a desire for a different, perhaps better, home and/or neighbourhood. While the probability of such moves is age-related, Cribier argues that the primary motivation for the move is one shared by all ages and is not a function of aging, per se. Lastly, Cribier discusses seasonal and temporary moves. This form of migration is most closely related to retirement migration and tends to involve the younger elderly who are reasonably healthy and wealthy, and therefore able to engage in long, seasonal "vacations." Seasonal moves may precede permanent moves or may serve as a substitute.

In summary, migration is closely related to chronological age and to passage through the lifecourse. Elderly migration tends to peak around the retirement age when recently retired elderly persons are most likely to engage in amenity or return migration. There is evidence that the elderly are becoming increasingly mobile in industrialized countries, especially around the age of retirement. Elderly migration tends to rise somewhat in the later years as the very old become more at risk for, and experience forced moves into institutional or other care-giving settings. Nevertheless, the elderly do show a high degree of residential stability, and only a minority change their residence in any given five-year period of time.

THE EFFECTS OF AGE ON THE PROBABILITY OF MOVING

Figure 4.1 shows the probability of moving at least once in the 1976–81 time period. These data are presented for males and females of all ages (five to eighty-five and older). While Canadians of all ages are more likely to move shorter distances than longer distances, nevertheless, the probabilities of making local, non-local intraprovincial and interprovincial moves have very similar patterns across the life span. Mobility is high for young adults, and also for young children as a consequence of the high mobility of parents in their twenties and thirties. Mobility tends to reach a temporary low about the age of seventeen as maturing families become less likely to move for both reasons of job and family security and stability. However, once young adults pass high school age, their propensity to leave home is dramatically evident. The tendency to move rises sharply in the young adult

FIGURE 4.1

THE PERCENTAGE OF MOVERS 1976–81 BY AGE, SEX AND TYPE OF MOVE

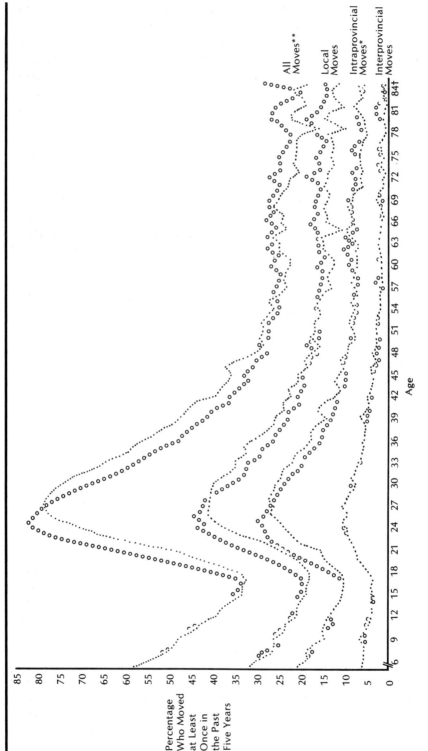

Percentage Who Moved at Least Once in the Past Five Years

Age

All Moves**

Local Moves

Intraprovincial Moves*

Interprovincial Moves

Legend: Male···· Female ∘∘∘∘

* excludes local moves.   **excludes international moves.   †85+

Source: The 1981 Public Use Sample Tape (2 percent sample), The Census of Canada

years, peaking in the mid-twenties for females and about two years later for males. From these peaks in the mid-twenties, the probability of residential change declines greatly before levelling of in the mid-forties, and declining very gradually with increasing years. While the elderly are less likely to move than any other age group, nevertheless, significant proportions of the elderly do change their place of residence. While these data are suggestive of the tendency to move at any point in the life span, remember that these data reflect different persons of varying age and do not follow the same people over their individual life spans.

While the patterns of mobility by age are very similar for males and females, the male and female curves for local and non-local intraprovincial moves diverge somewhat following high school age, with males being somewhat less likely to move. Females, perhaps, seek their independence earlier than their male peers, and tend to marry earlier. As a consequence, male mobility peaks several years later than female mobility. However, male mobility exceeds female mobility from its peak in the late twenties through the mid-forties. From the mid-forties to the end of life, male mobility for local and intraprovincial moves tends to drop below the levels of female mobility, and this is especially true for local moves. With respect to interprovincial migration, male and female patterns remain very similar for all ages.

MOBILITY ACROSS THE GENERATIONS

The 1981 Elderly Cohort: Lifetime Migration

According to the 1981 Census, 70 percent of the persons aged sixty-five and older living in Canada were born in Canada. Of the remaining 30 percent, most are immigrants from Europe and to a lesser degree from the United States, with smaller numbers originating in Asia, South and Central America, Africa and elsewhere. Note that these data do not indicate the percentages of the Canadian-born or foreign-born elderly populations that have emigrated from Canada.

With respect to the 30 percent of the elderly population who were born outside of Canada but who were resident in Canada in 1981, two-thirds had come to Canada before 1946 and fully 80 percent had arrived before 1956. In other words, 80 percent had lived in Canada for the last twenty-five years or more. Only 4 percent of Canada's elderly had immigrated in the 1976–81 period. These data mean, of course, that most of our elderly immigrants came at relatively young ages. Indeed, 40 percent of Canada's elderly immigrants came years ago as children (from zero to nineteen years of age), almost one-quarter arrived when they were young adults (twenty to thirty-four years of age) and almost one-third arrived in their middle years (thirty-five to sixty-four years of age). Less than 6 percent of Canada's elderly immigrants were sixty-five years of age and older when they first came to live in this country.

Turning to the Canadian-born population aged sixty-five and older, fully 80 percent of Canada's elderly in 1981 resided in the province of their birth. This statistic suggests a rather high level of retention (that is, immobility) at the provincial level; however, there are considerable variations from province to province.[1] At one extreme, the provinces of Quebec, Ontario, and British Columbia have retained 90 percent, 89 percent, and 88 percent, respectively, of their native-born elderly populations. At the other extreme, for those elderly persons born in the Prairie Provinces, only 48 percent of the native-born still remain in Saskatchewan, while 54 percent and 64 percent of Manitobans and Albertans continue to reside in their home provinces. Between these two extremes, the Atlantic Provinces have retained between 73 percent and 79 percent of their native-born older residents.

The preceding paragraph discussed the percentage of elderly born in a given province who still reside in that province. The following discussion turns the analysis around and examines the origins of elderly persons currently living in a given province. In other words, the first issue focuses on retention while the second issue goes beyond retention to examine attraction. These data are presented in Table 4.1 and clearly show that some provinces have been more attractive to migrants than other provinces.

At one extreme is Newfoundland, where 97 percent of elderly residents are native born. In other words, Newfoundland has had virtually no enduring attraction for the residents of other provinces or, indeed, for immigrants to Canada. At the other extreme is British Columbia, where only 16 percent of elderly residents are native born. In British Columbia, 38 percent of the elderly have arrived from other Canadian provinces, and 45 percent have come from other countries. Like British Columbia, significant percentages of the elderly populations of Ontario and the Prairie Provinces are foreign born, in contrast to the relatively small foreign-born percentages of the elderly populations of Quebec and the Atlantic Provinces.

By placing the above observations regarding retention and attraction together, we can see that 90 percent of elderly persons born in Quebec have remained in that province, while 81 percent of the elderly currently living in Quebec are native born. Ontario, on the other hand, has retained almost the same percentage of native-born elderly as Quebec (89 percent), but of those elderly currently living in Ontario, only 52 percent are native born. In other words, while both Ontario and Quebec have similar rates of retention, these two provinces differ noticeably in their ability to attract persons from out-of-province, with Ontario being the more attractive. The same point can be made even more strongly for British Columbia which has retained 88 percent of its native-born elderly, but which can claim that only 16 percent of its elderly population were born there. Clearly, British Columbia has had, and continues to have, a very strong appeal for Canadians.

TABLE 4.1

THE GEOGRAPHIC ORIGINS OF PERSONS SIXTY-FIVE YEARS OF AGE AND OLDER, BY PROVINCE OF RESIDENCE, 1981

Province of Residence	Percentage of the Elderly Born in Province of Current Residence (%)	Percentage of the Elderly Born Outside Province of Current Residence		Total	
		In Canada (%)	Outside Canada (%)	(%)[1]	(N)
Newfoundland	97	1	1	99	820
Prince Edward Island[2]	83	10	7	100	318
Nova Scotia	82	11	8	101	1,753
New Brunswick	83	11	7	101	1,318
Quebec	81	5	14	100	10,519
Ontario	52	11	38	101	16,084
Manitoba	56	11	33	100	2,256
Saskatchewan	50	17	33	100	2,150
Alberta	31	24	45	100	2,931
British Columbia	16	38	45	99	5,518
Total	56	14	30	100	43,667

1. Differences from 100 percent are due to rounding errors.
2. Includes the Yukon and Northwest Territories. Prince Edward Island and the Territories are combined by Statistics Canada to protect confidentiality.

SOURCE: The 1981 Public Use Sample Tape (2 percent sample), The 1981 Census of Canada.

Comparisons of Elderly Cohorts (1981, 1976, 1971, and 1961)

Are successive generations of the elderly becoming more (or less) mobile? Do successive generations of movers have the same (or different) origins and destinations? Or to put these questions more specifically, one might ask whether Canada's elderly population is increasingly likely to move to British Columbia? These questions have been addressed previously in two papers (Northcott 1985, 1984a) which are now reviewed.

First, with respect to the issue of increasing mobility, relevant data are provided by the question, "Where did you live five years ago?" which was asked in the 1961, 1971, 1976, and 1981 Censuses. An analysis of these data shows increasing mobility from 1961 to 1971 for both elderly and non-elderly Canadians and for both short- and long-distance moves. Non-elderly mobility continued to increase from 1971 to 1981, while the elderly showed an increase only in interprovincial migration. Levels of intraprovincial mobility for the elderly in 1981 dropped back to near 1961 levels (Northcott 1985, 188).

While these data cannot clearly indicate long-term trends, nevertheless, they do suggest that Canadians generally are increasingly likely to change their place of residence and that the elderly, more specifically, are increasingly likely to change their province of residence. Just the same, interprovincial moves are relatively rare.

The second question concerns the origins and destinations of successive generations of elderly Canadians. Throughout the 1961 to 1981 period, the cities of Victoria, Vancouver, Calgary, and Edmonton continued to be especially attractive to elderly migrants from other provinces (Northcott 1985, 191). An analysis of interprovincial migration comparing 1961 and 1976 cohorts (Northcott 1984a, 8–9) shows that about 1.5 percent of elderly persons sixty-five and older in 1961 changed their province of residence during 1956–61, while about 1.7 percent moved interprovincially in 1971–76. In both periods of time, British Columbia attracted more elderly migrants (mostly from the Prairies and from Ontario) than any other single province; British Columbia and Ontario together attracted over half of the older interprovincial migrants; Quebec continued to lose elderly persons to Ontario, while Manitoba lost elderly residents to Ontario, Alberta, and British Columbia; Manitoba, Saskatchewan, and Quebec were heavy net losers while British Columbia and Ontario were significant net gainers; and, finally, there were no significant net exchanges between the Atlantic Provinces and the western provinces. Despite the persistence of these patterns, from 1956–61 to 1971–76, there were also some notable changes in elderly interprovincial migration patterns including an increasing tendency for the Atlantic Provinces to show net gains of elderly persons from Quebec and Ontario, a substantial increase in the net movement of elderly females from Manitoba to Ontario, an end to Saskatchewan's net loss to Ontario, and the increasing attraction of British Columbia for the elderly from Ontario and

Quebec. With regards to the sex ratio of migrants (Northcott 1984a, 9), British Columbia, from 1961 to 1976, has tended to attract, in net, more elderly males than elderly females. This suggests that retiring couples (the male is usually older than his spouse) are a major component of the migration streams into that province. Ontario, on the other hand shows an increasingly discrepant sex ratio as net migration streams (mostly from Quebec and Manitoba) have become disproportionately female, thereby suggesting that Ontario is especially attractive to elderly widows from neighbouring provinces.

IMPLICATIONS FOR THE FUTURE

The decision to change the place of one's residence depends on many factors, and it is therefore difficult to predict future migration patterns with any certainty. Nevertheless, past trends may be suggestive of future patterns. For subsequent generations of elderly Canadians, shorter-distance moves will continue to outnumber more-distant moves. Given continued improvements in health, life expectancy, and the economic status of the elderly, it is anticipated that increasingly healthy and wealthy cohorts of elderly persons will take increasing advantage of their opportunities to move to a desirable place to live. That is, it is anticipated that amenity-drawn migration — primarily to British Columbia and southern Ontario — of couples who are increasingly likely to survive together well into their retirement years, will continue to increase. Indeed, as the elderly population becomes a growth industry, one would expect that both short- and long-distance moves to retirement communities or to housing complexes for the elderly will become more common in Canada. Forced moves into institutional housing, because of declining health and/or wealth, will continue to accompany the end of life for some, although such moves may tend to come later in the life span.[2] Indeed, forced moves into institutions may decline as social services such as home care, day care, meals-on-wheels, et cetera, develop, and as alternatives such as retirement apartment complexes, "granny flats," and so on, become increasingly available. In short, a healthier and wealthier elderly population will be increasingly mobile and increasingly likely to make moves of preference.

NOTES

1. Note that these statistics ignore elderly persons born in Canada who now reside outside of Canada.
2. This last point assumes a compression of the period of morbidity preceding death into fewer and fewer of the last years of life (see Fries 1983).

CHAPTER 5

THE MOBILITY PATTERNS OF ELDERLY POPULATIONS IN DEVELOPED COUNTRIES

Previous chapters have examined the mobility patterns of older Canadians. Population aging, however, is occurring in all of the industrialized nations. Indeed, a number of the developed countries currently have populations with a much higher proportion of elderly than does Canada. It is important to know whether Canada's experience with its own aging population is unique, or similar to other industrialized nations. If similar, then the experience of other "aged" countries can help us to better understand and predict the growth, mobility patterns, and needs of future cohorts of older Canadians. This chapter, then, examines the age structures and elderly migration patterns of the United States, Britain, France, and Australia.[1] Similarities and differences between these countries and Canada will be noted, as well as the implications for Canada.

THE UNITED STATES

In 1982, the elderly age group in the United States comprised 11.6 percent of the total population (United Nations 1985, 200). By comparison, Canada in 1982 was just approaching the 10 percent level. In the past, for several reasons, very little attention has been paid, in the United States and elsewhere, to the elderly mover. First, the elderly constituted only a small percentage of the population, and second, the elderly constituted an even smaller percentage of the geographically mobile. Nevertheless, many elderly persons do change their place of residence and, with the increase in the proportion of elderly in the population, attention has begun to be paid to the elderly mover. Attention has focused on the probability of various kinds of moves, on the choice of destination, on the characteristics and needs of the elderly mover, and on the implications for the sending and receiving communities. Indeed, a rather substantial literature has emerged in the last decade or so examining the phemonenon of elderly migration in the United States.

The United States Bureau of the Census (1984, 31) reports that there are wide variations from state to state in the proportion of the population which is elderly — ranging in 1980 from 2.9 percent in Alaska to 17.3 percent in Florida. The proportion of elderly persons depends largely on fertility and migration. States with high fertility (for example, Utah) and states with high in-migration of young persons (for example, Colorado) tend to have relatively low proportions of elderly. States with low fertility and high out-migration of young persons (for example, much of the midwestern farm belt) have relatively high proportions of elderly residents. States with high in-migration of elderly adults (for example, Florida) also have relatively high proportions of elderly residents. Turning from the proportion of the elderly in the total population to the growth rate of the elderly population itself, states in the South and West (for example, Florida and Arizona, where elderly in-migration is high) have relatively high rates of growth, while states in the North (for example, New York) have low rates of growth. These patterns, based on 1980 census data, are very similar to patterns observed in the 1960 census data (Rogers 1974).

While there is considerable variation from state to state, there is even greater variation among counties. Many counties in states with high proportions of aged persons have populations which are over 20 percent elderly; indeed, several counties in Florida have in excess of 30 percent. While the elderly are less likely than the general population to move, and even less likely (less than half as likely) to move long distances, nevertheless, there are significant movements of elderly persons between states. New York, for example, loses heavily to other states while the Sunbelt states of Florida, Texas, Arizona, and California gain heavily (United States Bureau of the Census 1984, 33).

The elderly are not as mobile as are the non-elderly (see, for example, Longino and Biggar 1981, 283); nevertheless, when the non-elderly and the elderly move, both are more likely to move short distances rather than long distances. For the elderly, long-distance moves are often associated with retirement and may involve a return to the state of birth, a move to a more attractive locale (for example, to Florida or the rural fringe around a major city or to a retirement community), or a move to be near kin. Of course, not all long-distance moves are permanent, and there is a significant degree of seasonal migration involving, for example, elderly "snowbirds" who move south for the winter to escape the cold northern climate (Hoyt 1954; Sullivan and Stevens 1982; Krout 1983; Hogan 1987; Martin et al. 1987). There may also be a seasonal flow in the summer as southern residents move northwards to escape the heat of summer. Such a pattern, however, has not yet been documented (although consider Sullivan 1985).

Serow (1978; see also Longino and Biggar 1981, 287–89) assessed the return migration of elderly Americans for 1955–60 and 1965–70. Serow notes that only a small percentage of returning migrants are elderly; that is, most returnees are non-elderly. Just the same, Serow points out that in comparison to non-elderly migration, return migration is a larger component and an increasingly important component of elderly migration. Indeed, for all American elderly migrants, 18 percent were return migrants in 1955–60 and 22 percent in 1965–70 (Serow 1978, 290). Return migration streams, of course, reflect the migrants' birth places; that is, elderly return migration is high in the Northeast and in the Midwest where many elderly Americans were born. On the other hand, elderly return migration is low in the mountain and Pacific states where comparably few elderly Americans were born. Elderly return migration as a proportion of all in-migration is also low in Florida where non-returning elderly in-migrants are numerous. Elderly migrants are more likely to return to their state of birth if that state is a popular destination such as Florida or Arizona; of course, non-native elderly are also likely to migrate to such attractive areas. Given that all states experience a degree of return migration, areas that have had a high out-migration of young people may yet experience significant returns of elderly as the population ages (Serow 1978, 294–95).

Chevan and Fischer (1979, 1370) also observe that elderly persons who are not resident in their state of birth have a propensity to return home near the time of retirement. Nevertheless, Chevan and Fischer (1979, 1366), using 1970 census data, note that about one-half of all retired migrants moved to either Florida, Arizona, or California. Indeed, Longino and Biggar (1981, 284–86) report that Florida attracts one-fourth of elderly inter-state migrants, California draws one-tenth, and Arizona and Texas are becoming increasingly popular retirement destinations. Further, Florida tended to draw migrants from the eastern half of the United States while Arizona and California drew heavily from the western half. These patterns continued more or less through the 1975–80 period (Flynn et al. 1985), with retirement migration becoming increasingly common, and with Florida, Arizona, and Texas becoming increasingly popular destinations. California, while a popular destination, also had a significant counterstream of elderly out-migrants; indeed, California lost almost as many elderly as it gained. These elderly out-migrants from California may include previous in-migrants returning home, persons discouraged by California's congestion and high cost of living, and persons attracted to popular nearby states such as Arizona, Nevada, and Oregon. North Carolina and the state of Washington are also rapidly gaining popularity. New York remains the leading state of origin; however, New Jersey is declining in importance as a destination for elderly New Yorkers.

With respect to the characteristics of migrants, those elderly Americans engaging in interstate migration tend to be retired rather than working, younger, married, in good health, of higher socio-economic status (with higher occupational status, more education, higher pre- and post-retirement incomes), to have been migrants previously, and to originate in the more northerly Snowbelt states and to be bound for the Sunbelt, that is, for the warmer and sunnier coastal, desert, and mountain states in the South and

Southwest (Chevan and Fischer 1979; Biggar 1980; Biggar et al. 1980; Longino and Biggar 1981, 284–86).

Not all elderly migration in the United States is directed to the Sunbelt. For example, there is evidence that non-metropolitan counties generally are becoming increasingly attractive to elderly migrants seeking to escape the environment of the large city; indeed, retirement migration has played a role in the "rural-urban turnaround" (Heaton et al. 1980, 1981; Kim and Hartwigsen 1983; Frey 1986). Of course, many of these attractive non-metropolitan counties are in the South and many others are within easy driving distance of large metropolitan complexes.

Recent decades have witnessed the emergence of privately developed (as opposed to government-sponsored) retirement communities, not only in the South and Southwest but also in the Midwest and Northwest (Heintz 1976). Many of these communities are located on metropolitan fringes. One of the largest Sunbelt retirement communities is Sun City, Arizona, founded in the 1960s (Gober and Zonn 1983). Sun City is adjacent to Phoenix, and in 1980 had a population of forty-five thousand. Sun City West is currently under construction and anticipates a population of seventy-five thousand residents. Of course, many retirement communities are on a much smaller scale and range in nature from trailer parks to condominiums to single-family housing neighbourhoods.

A third form of retirement migration, besides movement to return home or to improve life-style, is kinship migration; that is, a move to live with, or more often, to be near family members (Wiseman and Roseman 1979). Of course, these three forms of migration may overlap. Elderly people are more likely to return home if their home state offers an attractive life-style (Heaton et al. 1981), and kinship and life-style migration are often linked (Gober and Zonn 1983).

The patterns of elderly migration in the United States raise several issues including age-segregation, housing pressures, and impact on local (for example, social and medical) services. La Gory et al. (1980, 74–74) note that, in areas such as the northeastern and the north-central states, the elderly tend to age in place, and age-segration is a consequence of the out-migration of the non-elderly. In the Sunbelt areas of the South and the West, age-segregation and also competition for housing often result as a consequence of the in-migration of elderly. While the heavy in-migration of the elderly to states such as Florida and Arizona results in concentrations of older persons, because these in-migrants are the younger segments of the retired population, and are relatively healthy and wealthy, they put little negative pressure on local services and indeed, as consumers, add to the local economy. Nevertheless, in time, these migrants age and become increasingly at risk with respect to economic and/or health dependency (Bryant and El-Attar 1984; see also Longino and Biggar 1982).

Elderly American migration patterns have many parallels with Canadian patterns. First of all, the channelized streams of elderly interstate migrants moving from the Snowbelt to the Sunbelt states of Florida, California, and Arizona are perhaps similar, though on a larger scale, to the movement of elderly Canadians from the Prairies to milder British Columbia. Second, Canada like the States, exhibits evidence of significant streams of return migrants to most provinces, but especially to the more attractive provinces such as Ontario or those of the Maritimes. Third, it is likely that in Canada, as in the States, movement to be near kin is a significant pattern. Fourth, there is evidence that elderly interprovincial migration (retirement migration) is increasing in Canada (Northcott 1985), as it is in the United States, and is highly selective both in terms of destination (British Columbia, Ontario) and migrant characteristics (younger, healthier, wealthier, and more educated). Fifth, in Canada, as in the States, there are concerns about the redistribution of the elderly population resulting in concentrations in selected provinces and in selected locales with implications for the demand for services, especially for senior citizen housing and for medical, hospital and nursing home care. Sixth, while both Canada and the States have their "snowbirds," a significant difference between the two countries concerns the international nature of Canada's seasonal migration patterns; that is, Canada has a significant pattern of seasonal migrants crossing the border to spend part or all of the winter in the American Sunbelt. Indeed, as in the United States, eastern Canadians often travel to Florida and western Canadians to Arizona and California. Finally, it remains to be seen whether or not the United States phenomenon of private-sector development of retirement communities will occur to a similar extent in Canada. Given the close parallels between the two countries with respect to elderly migration, and given the tendency for American innovations to diffuse in time into Canada (our universal health care program is a notable exception), it seems likely that private developers will become increasingly cognizant of the market opportunities that the elderly retiree represents. A final question remains concerning the movement of the elderly from the large central cities to small towns and rural areas (often on the fringes of large metropolitan complexes). As noted in Chapter 3, Canada's larger cities do tend to show a net loss of elderly persons due to migration. Just the same, while acreages and satellite towns near metropolitan centres have their appeal, it is not at all clear that Canada's cities exhibit the same "push" as do the older and larger American urban centres.

BRITAIN

Britain's population is substantially older than the populations of Canada or the United States. In 1982, 15.2 percent of the population of England and Wales was sixty-five years of age and older (United Nations 1985, 214). By contrast, the elderly in the United States in 1982 stood at 11.6 percent while

Canada's elderly reached the 10.0 percent level in 1983 (United Nations 1985, 196, 200). For some time now, researchers in Britain have been concerned with the high proportion of elderly, and with the concentrating and segregating effects of the migration of retired persons and the consequent implications for housing and other local services.

Mellor (1962) examined the movement of elderly retirees to the coastal areas of England and Wales. His study showed that, for a sample of nine seaside resorts in 1951, the elderly were significantly overrepresented, constituting one and a half to two times the percentage of the elderly in the general population. Mellor argues that the large, heavily industrialized cities are relatively unattractive to elderly retirees and that retired couples often relocate to seaside resorts. Oftentimes, the resort chosen as a retirement residence has been a frequent holiday locale and tends to be relatively close to the city of employment, though many do travel longer distances. For example, the south coast of England attracts people from all over the country. In other words, the push of the industrial city and the pull of the seaside resort draw many elderly retirees to the coast.[2] In these seaside resorts then, the proportion of residents who are elderly is high and, accordingly, death rates are high and birth rates low. Given that high death rates and low birth rates imply declining population size in the absence of migration, the stable or growing populations in the seaside resorts suggest high rates of continuing in-migration by the elderly (Mellor 1962, 40).

Mellor suggests that the phenomenon of elderly retirement to coastal resorts could be used to alleviate "overspill problems," (that is, to relieve the congestion and housing pressure in the industrial cities). In 1951, elderly coastal retirees tended to be couples who had the means to buy accommodation. Renters often ran the risk of being displaced from their rooms during the holiday season when landlords preferred to raise rents. Mellor argues that a policy to provide secure rental accommodation in seaside resorts would tend to draw even more elderly and would thereby alleviate, to a degree, the housing problems in the cities.

Of course, high concentrations of elderly persons raise concerns about the ability of the local community to provide and pay for services that the elderly require. Mellor (1962, 48) suggests that these concerns are unwarranted inasmuch as the proportion of elderly residents is unlikely to rise much higher, the elderly themselves pay local taxes, and central government block grants to local communities are (or may be) adjusted for the proportion of elderly people in the local area.

It is important to distinguish the migration of retired persons, generally, from migration which specifically follows the event of retirement. Law and Warnes (1973) focus on the latter in their study of the movement of retired persons to two seaside resorts, Llandudno on the north coast of Wales and Morecambe on England's northwest coast. Both of these towns are relatively close to the major industrial cities of Liverpool and Manchester. And these two seaside resorts serve as retirement centres; in 1966, for example, the elderly constituted 25 percent of the population of Morecambe. Law and Warnes surveyed the populations of these two towns in 1970–71 and compared employed migrants, retired migrants, and non-migrants. The authors found that retired migrants tended to be couples, of higher socio-economic status, to have moved more in the past, to have vacationed at the resort, and to have originated in the industrial cities less than a hundred miles distant. Law and Warnes (1973, 382, 384) suggest that the "pull" factors associated with the seaside resorts were stronger motivation for retirement migration than the "push" factors associated with the industrial cities from whence the migrants originated. Law and Warnes (1973, 387) note that their study supports "the belief that retirement migration will become a mass movement, like many other manifestations of an affluent and leisure-conscious society." However, the authors suggest that the destinations chosen for retirement will change with the times, although there will continue to be preference for rural and/or waterside and/or hilly or mountainous locations. Finally, Law and Warnes (1973, 387–88) speculate, that as people become more and more widely travelled, retirement migration will be of increasingly longer distances, perhaps developing a significant international component, with people moving not only to their own country's amenity areas but also to other nations' more desirable places.

Lemon (1973) discusses the impact of retirement migration on thirty-one small towns in Norfolk and Suffolk counties, England, for the period from 1961 to 1966. Lemon (1973, 259–60) notes that the coastal resorts, as well as the more attractive inland towns and those towns offering attractive housing tailored to the needs of retirees, are most successful in attracting the elderly. Indeed, most of the small towns have disproportionately high percentages of elderly due to the in-migration of retired persons and the out-migration of young persons. With respect to the social and economic impact of elderly in-migration, Lemon (1973, 260–61) notes that there are pluses — the in-coming elderly offset population losses and add money to the local economy, and minuses — the elderly may put a strain on hospital and medical services, and do not constitute a labour force that will attract the industry that, Lemon argues, may, in the long term, be essential to the survival of the small towns. Lemon perhaps underestimates the rise of post-industrial economies based on services. It may be that the elderly as consumers of services might well attract and/or hold a local work force. In other words, retirement might well become an "industry" in its own right.

Sant (1977, 248–58), in his analysis of the geography of retirement in Britain in 1961–71, notes the attraction of the south coast for retirees from the southern metropolitan areas, and of the coast of northern Wales and northern England for retirees from metropolitan centres in northwest England. In contrast, the high proportion of retirees in central Wales was primarily a function of the out-migration of young adults — the in-migration stream of retirees being rather modest by comparison. Sant also notes concentrations of retirees in selected areas of the east coast and in areas peripheral to major metropolitan areas. Few retirees appeared to migrate to the remoter rural areas of Wales or Scotland. Most of the retired migrants originated in the larger cities and travelled relatively short distances.

These British studies of retirement migration have focused not only on the origins and destinations of elderly persons but also on policy implications, especially with respect to housing. A more recent study by Warnes and Law (1985) continues this emphasis. These authors observe that the rapid aging of the population, and in particular the increase in the seventy-five years and older group, means increasing demand for retirement housing and accommodation for the widowed and the frail elderly. Further, the tendency for elderly retirees to concentrate in selected areas — traditionally the seaside resorts and, more recently, attractive inland locations — suggests that elderly housing needs will be particularly pressing for certain local areas. Warnes and Law (1985, 294) note that the elderly have been increasingly mobile and increasingly likely to move longer distances. In the past, retirees tended to move, for example, to nearby seaside resorts. Now, the elderly are more likely to move to more distant locales. For example, northern retirees are now more likely to move to the south coast. Of course, not all elderly migration is for life-style reasons, and shorter-distance moves still predominate over longer moves. Housing shortages and the high cost of housing in seaside resorts, coupled with the development of inland areas, have encouraged elderly migrants increasingly to settle in attractive inland locations. Warnes and Law (1985, 296) list twenty county districts in which pensionable populations (males over sixty-five and females over sixty) constitute more than one-quarter to one-third of the resident population. In accordance with past patterns of migration, those county districts with high proportions of elderly residents tend to be located along the coasts, especially along the southern third of Britian, (that is, the south coast, and the coasts of Wales and East Anglia). Nevertheless, the authors note (page 298) that in the 1971–81 decade the elderly have shown a tendency towards increasing dispersion, thereby reversing the 1951–71 trend towards selective concentration. Warnes and Law note, that in areas where young people have been out-migrating, the proportion of elderly tends to be high, although declining in absolute number. Where there has been a high in-migration of elderly persons, to seaside resorts for example, that has not been replenished by recent high levels of elderly in-migration (due to high costs, housing shortages, restrictive policies), then these elderly populations become increasingly old, frail, and widowed. The authors (page 303) suggest that, providing the elderly can sell their homes at a favourable price, and providing that they can find attractive housing, then, with rising economic prosperity and with the aging of the baby boom, there should be high rates of elderly migration resulting in substantial concentrations of the elderly in selected locales, thus resulting in high levels of age segregation.

British retirement migration has implications for Canada. Given that Britain is ahead of Canada in terms of population aging, Britain's experience with retirement migration may be instructive. The increasing rates of elderly mobility, together with the tendency to move longer distances, has been and is likely to continue to be reflected in Canada's experience (Northcott 1985). Nevertheless, in Canada as in Britain, shorter-distance moves predominate and will continue to do so. Migration to take advantage of the amenities offered in popular and attractive locations is significant in both Britain and Canada; however, there are substantial differences between the two countries in this regard. First of all, while British amenity areas are often located within several hours drive of major cities, in Canada, amenity areas tend to be many hundreds and even thousands of miles distant from major cities. Because shorter moves predominate, this means that migration to amenity areas is a less significant part of the total elderly migration picture in Canada than in Britain. Second, while it is often the case in Britain that the elderly are attracted to a town or region from which the non-elderly are dispersing, in Canada, the elderly and non-elderly migration streams tend to be very similar, at the macro level at least (Northcott 1984a). However, an analysis of elderly and non-elderly migration by Canadian town and/or local region remains to be done. Certainly there are Canadian towns that attract elderly retirees, while at the same time dispersing younger residents. Nevertheless, at the larger level of analysis, British Columbia and southern Ontario are attractive to both elderly and non-elderly migrants. Because Canadian elderly and non-elderly migration streams tend to be similar, Canada has not experienced the concentration of the elderly (that is, the segregation of elderly persons), that Britain has. In 1981, 17 percent of the city of Victoria consisted of the elderly (Northcott 1984b, 42), and while this figure is high in the Canadian context, it is far from the 25 to 35 percent reported for some British towns.

Retirement migration in Canada appears to be less of a "mass phenomenon" than in Britain, although certainly there are significant levels of retirement migration. For Canada, as is becoming apparent in Britain, this retirement migration has an international component in terms of seasonal migrants to sunnier climes (Canada's winter "snowbirds" bound for the American Sunbelt, for example). Finally, formal housing policies for the non-institutionalized elderly appear to be less of an issue in Canada than in Britain, although continued population aging may yet bring this issue to the fore in Canada. At this point in time, government-sponsored programs to provide housing for elderly retirees in selected locations (as Mellor 1962 proposed) is likely to be seen as both unnecessary and, given the "ghettoization" overtones, undesirable. As has happened in recent years in Britain, the private sector is discovering the market for the elderly and increasingly providing not only housing but also entire communities tailored to the needs and preferences of the older, non-institutionalized population.

FRANCE

In 1983, 13.2 percent of the population of France was sixty-five years of age and older (United Nations 1985, 210), ahead of Canada's 10.0 percent, but behind the English and Welsh population which was over 15 percent. Cribier (1975, 361) notes that in the past the geographic distribution of the elderly in France was primarily a function of the birth rate and the movement of younger persons. Increasingly, however, the geographic movement of the elderly themselves is shaping their spatial distribution in France. Cribier observes that in the 1960s the elderly were about one-half as likely to move as the general population — indeed, the majority did not move. Nevertheless, many elderly persons did change their place of residence by moving near the time of their retirement or moving later in life as circumstances of declining health or economics forced a move into a nursing home, hospital, or the home of one of their children (Cribier 1975, 363). Focusing on retirement migration, Cribier (1975; see also 1980) observes that in France there are two main types of retirement moves: migration involving movement to attractive locales, and return migration involving moves from cities of employment back to the place from whence the person originated years ago. These return moves are primarily to smaller towns and rural areas.

In France, return migration tends to disperse migrants widely from the large cities. Cribier (1975, 366, 372; 1980, 267) notes that the current generation of older persons, many of whom have migrated to Paris from diverse origins in France, are especially likely to leave Paris on retirement and to return to their various places of origin. In contrast to return migration, migration to amenity areas is more selective with migrants choosing to move to the more attractive destinations. Further, the retiree's social class influences the tendency to move and the type of move undertaken (Cribier 1975; 1980, 264). The wealthier retirees in the upper and upper-middle classes in the large cities, such as Paris, are more likely to have carved out a comfortable niche in the city and are more likely to be able to continue to afford city living. Consequently, the wealthier classes in the larger cities are less likely to move than are the poor classes (the lower-middle, working, and lower classes), who tend to find city living expensive and often return to their home towns or regions where the cost of living is more favourable. Further, the wealthier retired urbanites may be less likely to move because they may have a second home in an amenity area and are more likely to engage in seasonal migration (for example, the wealthy might winter on the Riviera and/or summer elsewhere at the seaside or in the country). When these wealthier elderly do make a permanent retirement move, they tend to migrate to favoured destinations such as resort towns on the Atlantic and Mediterranean coasts or to attractive inland areas such as the Basque countryside. For the poor, migration to attractive and popular locations is a less likely alternative, because of relatively high costs of living.

In short, France and Britain are alike in that both countries have large elderly populations with a rather high propensity to move at retirement. Both countries have significant streams of amenity-drawn migrants and, for both, such migrants tend to be the younger, married elderly, to be of higher social status (better educated, wealthier) and to have worked in large urban centres. Nevertheless, France and Britain differ in that France has a strong pattern of return migration which sees the less wealthy elderly leave the large cities to return to the regions of their birth. In both countries, the provision of services to the elderly is seen as a policy problem. In Britain, the high proportions of elderly in selected towns threaten to overwhelm local service capabilities while in France the dispersal of the elderly to rural areas where services are scarce presents a related problem.

The migration patterns in France have implications for Canada. First of all, France's patterns of retirement migration suggest that migration near the time of retirement may become more evident in Canada. Second, the phenomenon of migration to selected popular locations, already evident in Canada, may come to be accompanied more and more by the phenomenon of return migration. At present, while return migration exists in Canada, levels seem to be very modest in comparison to France. Further, the high concentrations of the elderly in small towns in Canada are more a function of the out-migration of the young and the movement of rural retirees to nearby centres than the return of expatriates from the major cities. Finally, Canada's elderly may find the cities more affordable than the elderly of France's larger cities. That is, many of France's poorer elderly migrants are driven from the city by high costs and attracted to rural home regions precisely because costs are lower. In Canada, there may be less of a differential between the cost of living in the city as opposed to a rural area or small town, and certainly the shortage of services in less urban areas is a disincentive to moving to such places. Or saying this differently, Canadians may be more urbanized — indeed Cribier (1975, 365) notes that in the industrialized, urbanized parts of northern France and Alsace there is not a tradition of "going back to the country." Canada may also, generally speaking, lack such a tradition. In short, it seems that in Canada, because there is less pressure on housing in both urban centres and in amenity areas, it is unlikely that a strong pattern of return retirement migration will develop.

AUSTRALIA

In 1981, the elderly in Australia, as in Canada, made up 9.7 percent of the population (United Nations 1985, 214). Murphy (1979, 84), writing of Australia, notes that the aging of the population coupled with the phenomenon of retirement migration makes social planners "particularly concerned to predict the future amount and location of elderly migrants and to assess ... the social and economic impacts ..." of elderly in-migration in order to design appropriate policies and to provide suitable facilities. Murphy (1979, 87–89) notes the attraction of warmer climates for retired people. In Australia, Queensland's Gold Coast in the North (remember that in Australia, a move north is a move to a sunnier and warmer climate) compares with the American Sunbelt states of Florida, Arizona, and California, and with Canada's British Columbia. Nevertheless, Murphy notes that the great bulk of moves are of shorter rather than longer distance. In New South Wales, most of the population is concentrated in the Newcastle-Sydney-Wollongong area, and elderly retirees tend to move primarily to nearby coastal areas or to own second homes along the coastal urban fringes. To a somewhat lesser degree, elderly retirees concentrate on the more distant coast north of Newcastle, notably in towns such as Port Macquarie, Coffs Harbour, Ballina, and Tweed Heads.

In short, while the elderly often do not move, when they do change their place of residence, shorter-distance moves tend to predominate. Nevertheless, when elderly retirees do move (either short or long distances), the attraction of coastal and of sunnier, warmer locations is once again evident.

SUMMARY

In summary, in terms of the proportion of the population which is elderly, Canada compares with Australia and lags behind the United States, France, and especially Britain. These five countries all appear to have increasingly significant streams of elderly, mobile retirees. Those recently retired elderly who are younger rather than older, healthy, of higher socio-economic status, married, and who have a history of prior mobility have a tendency to make a retirement move to an attractive location. These moves are usually in the direction of the sun and often also in the direction of the sea. Canada's most popular areas are British Columbia and southern Ontario; the American Sunbelt includes Florida, Arizona, and California; Britain has the coastal areas, especially the south coast; French amenity seekers choose the Mediterranean and Atlantic coasts; and Australia's Sunbelt includes the Queensland Gold Coast and the north coast of New South Wales. In North America there is a tendency for these Sunbelt movers to originate in the Snowbelt, that is, in the United States' Midwest or Northeast and virtually anywhere in Canada.

The elderly of the large cities in all five of these countries have a tendency to leave the large urban centres for the non-metropolitan fringe, or to migrate further to attractive locations, or to return to the area of birth. Return migration is not inconsequential in the United States and is especially salient in France where the lower-middle and poorer classes exhibit a strong tendency to leave major cities to return to their more rural origins. In all five countries, these patterns of migration result in concentrations of elderly residents in selected attractive areas. France is an exception to a degree in that the return migration of the less wealthy classes is rather diffuse in destination, resulting in the dispersal rather than the concentration of the elderly.

The concentration of the aged population results not only from elderly migration, but also from the elderly population's tendency not to migrate. That is, in areas where the non-elderly are out-migrating (for example, central cities, rural regions), the elderly are often left behind. In short, the migration patterns of both the elderly and the non-elderly have a tendency to segregate and/or concentrate the elderly population into selected locations. These tendencies, evident in most industrialized countries, may present special problems for the provision of housing and for the delivery of services in local areas. The next chapter examines the policy implications of elderly migration in Canada.

NOTES

1. For a comprehensive review of the geography of aging, see Rowles 1986.
2. The situation may be the reverse for many young people who are drawn from smaller towns to the larger cities where employment prospects are higher.

CHAPTER 6

THE POLICY IMPLICATIONS OF ELDERLY MOBILITY

Policies established in such areas as health care, retirement, Old Age Security, and housing have implications for the geographic mobility of elderly Canadians. For example, the timing of retirement, the availability of affordable housing, and the portability of health care insurance and Old Age Security benefits all influence the decision to move, or not, and the choice of destination. Further, not only does policy influence geographic mobility, but the geographic mobility of the elderly population also has implications for policy. For example, geographic movement resulting in the concentration of the elderly in selected locales raises questions for housing policy and for health care delivery. This chapter, then, explores the implications of policy for geographic mobility and the implications of geographic mobility for policy.

THE IMPLICATIONS OF POLICY FOR GEOGRAPHIC MOBILITY

Retirement Policy

Retirement policy in Canada rests in both the private and public sectors and applies to workers both selectively and "universally." That is, a pension program may apply selectively to workers employed in a given industry by a specific employer or may apply "universally" as in the Canada Pension Plan where all employed persons who meet eligibility requirements qualify for benefits. Many employees participate in private sector (for example, IBM) or public sector (for example, civil service) employer-sponsored pension plans. Such plans often require retirement at a specific age (usually sixty-five), and offer benefits according to the years of service and level of income and therefore amount of contributions paid into the pension program. Withdrawal from the labour force, at, for example, age sixty-five, under programs such as these is referred to as mandatory retirement, although pension plans may have terms which allow for earlier voluntary retirement or for premature retirement forced by a disabling illness or condition. The future status of mandatory retirement in Canada is under some question at the time of writing. On the one hand, it is argued that the forced exclusion of persons of a certain age from employment constitutes discrimination on the basis of age and may violate either provincial and/or federal charters of rights. On the other hand, it is argued that employer-employee retirement pension agreements constitute valid contracts, the various charters of rights notwithstanding. In any case, retirement — whether forced or voluntary — is an event that may trigger a change of residence.

Labour force participation is an important factor constraining migration. Of course, local moves within the area of employment are not greatly influenced one way or another. Retirement, however, removes a major impediment to longer-distance moves. Further, while incomes tend to drop at retirement, nevertheless, receipt of a pension might still provide sufficient economic wherewithal to allow for a move. Given that pensions are generally paid to employees regardless of current residence, moving does not jeopardize pension income. Regardless of whether a person moves to the suburbs, to British Columbia, or to Florida, the pension cheque comes regularly in the mail.

Not all employers offer a pension plan, and benefits vary from employer to employer. Not all plans include survivor benefits, and the availability of pension incomes to widows is a factor in the mobility or immobility of this particular category of elderly Canadians.[1]

In order to provide all working Canadians and their dependents with a minimal level of pension income, the federal government began the Canada Pension Plan in 1966. Residents of Canada who have worked since 1966 for a minimum of ten years and paid the maximum level of contribution allowed are eligible at the age of sixty-five for the maximum benefit. Changes beginning in 1987 allow persons to continue paying into the plan up to the age of seventy and allow persons to elect to receive pension benefits beginning at any time between their sixtieth and seventieth birthdays.[2] Benefits are paid regardless of residence anywhere within or outside of Canada.

In short, while the level of pension income may discourage mobility, nevertheless, because pensions are paid regardless of place of residence, a person may move anywhere in the world without fear of losing the pension benefits. In addition, the pension can be made to "go further" by choosing a location in Canada or in another country where the cost of living is low. Places in Canada or other countries with high costs of living have the effect of reducing "pension" buying power and therefore of deterring in-migration.

Old Age Security

Residents who have lived in Canada for at least the last ten years are eligible to receive Old Age Security (OAS) payments monthly.[3] This benefit is payable anywhere in Canada and, anywhere in the world for elderly persons who leave the country for less than six months, or who leave permanently after living in Canada for at least twenty years following the attainment of age eighteen (Old Age Security Act 1984, 8). Because payment is made anywhere for the great majority of Canadian residents, there is no constraint on mobility. Further, as was the case with pension benefits, there is some motivation to move to places within Canada or to other countries where the cost of living is relatively low.

In addition to the Old Age Security benefit, elderly persons with low incomes are eligible for the Guaranteed Income Supplement (GIS).[4] A person who is sixty to sixty-four years of age and who is the spouse of a pensioner who receives the Guaranteed Income Supplement is eligible to receive the Spouse's Allowance (SPA).[5] Low-income, widowed persons between the ages of sixty and sixty-four are eligible to receive the Widowed Spouse's Allowance (WSPA).[6] All of these benefits — the GIS, SPA, and WSPA — are paid regardless of residence in Canada but cease when a person leaves Canada for a period exceeding six months (Old Age Security Act 1984, 10, 24). Consequently, these programs discourage the permanent movement of low-income elderly Canadians out of Canada, may encourage seasonal "snowbird" migration as an alternative to permanent emigration, and may encourage movement within Canada to regions where the cost of living is relatively modest.

Some Canadian provinces supplement the federal GIS benefit. These monthly benefits in 1985 ranged from a high of one hundred dollars per elderly GIS recipient in the Yukon Territory, and ninety-five dollars in Alberta, to nothing in Quebec, New Brunswick, Prince Edward Island, and Newfoundland. Provincial supplements to the federal GIS benefits, where paid, are lost when a person moves away from the given province and gained when a person moves permanently into that province. Alberta's subsidy may serve to retain low-income, elderly residents and to attract low-income, elderly persons from other provinces. Alternatively, Quebec's zero subsidy will not improve the attractiveness of that province relative to other provinces.

Health Care Insurance

Canada has had universal, comprehensive health care insurance for some time now. Every province provides coverage for basic hospital and medical expenses. Additional coverage varies from province to province (for a summary, see Health and Welfare Canada 1986a). Alberta, for example, provides Blue Cross and Extended Health Benefits programs, premium free, for all of its elderly residents. These benefits are portable within Canada, that is, a person who travels to another province retains insurance coverage. For a visitor from one province to another, under some circumstances, the traveller may have to pay for health care out-of-pocket and claim reimbursement from the home province. Alternatively, the province where treatment was provided may simply bill the home province. A person who changes province of residence permanently will apply to the new province for health care insurance coverage. In sum, health care policy presents little, if any, disincentive for movement within Canada.

In contrast, movement to places outside of Canada is far more problematic. While specific regulations vary from province to province, generally, a person's health care coverage is valid outside of Canada for a period of up to six months at one time or in any given year. However, it is usually the case that the visitor outside of Canada will pay out-of-pocket for health care expenses and will seek reimbursement from the home province. Further, reimbursement is typically at the home province's rate of payment, or otherwise limited, and visitors to the United States, for example, may find that there is a considerable difference between the American cost and the Canadian rate of reimbursement. Nevertheless, Canadians may purchase health insurance in Canada to cover health care costs incurred out-of-country, and Canadians resident in other countries may purchase health insurance locally, where available.

Canada's generally high quality of health care and the financial risks of illness occurring out-of-country are a strong incentive for elderly persons to remain within Canada. Even short-term or seasonal visitors to places outside of Canada run a risk, although the disincentive works most heavily against permanent out-migration and less heavily against seasonal or short-term international travellers.

Housing Policy

This discussion addresses several types of housing, including privately funded housing, publicly subsidized housing, and institutional housing such as homes for senior citizens.

Privately funded housing may be owned or rented, single-family homes, condominiums, or apartments, et cetera. Such facilities are offered for sale or rent by previous owners or by developers. Various policies govern site location, construction standards, and owner-tenant or seller-buyer agreements. These policies by themselves have little, if any, impact on the geographic movement of the elderly. However, the existence of these housing alternatives and their various costs may have considerable impact on elderly mobility. In other words, the rules of the marketplace, and in particular, the relationship of demand and supply, influence the decision to move, or not. Expensive housing will tend to act as a deterrent to elderly in-migration, for all but the most affluent. Further, expensive rental housing will tend to motivate the out-migration of elderly renters. Relatively inexpensive housing will tend to attract elderly buyers and renters, especially if that housing is located in desirable places.

Of course, the bulk of elderly movement covers relatively short, r₁ than long, distances. The elderly local mover may be retreating to the urbs or exurbs to escape the encroaching city centre, or may be changing homes in order to downsize and simplify his or her housing and its various burdens, or may be moving from a house to a condominium or apartment so as to both reduce the burden of upkeep and increase the opportunity for extended travel. In Edmonton, for example, Horizon Village Corporation began in 1983 to offer condominiums to persons aged fifty and older. By early 1987, Horizon Village Corporation had six "villages" in Edmonton, two in Calgary, and plans to expand to rural Alberta, and to Manitoba and Saskatchewan. Persons moving into Horizon Village range from the older employed person to the retiree, from the fifty-year-old to the person well into the seventies, and include both couples and singles. Most of these residents are local movers — that is, local persons who want to stay close to family and friends but who want to give up the old home with its present or potential burdens, and enjoy a less demanding housing alternative. Many also value the freedom to travel that condominium living provides.

In summary, the availability of affordable housing alternatives is an important factor in the local relocation of elderly persons. For elderly persons moving longer distances, again, the availability of affordable housing is an important consideration influencing the choice of destination.

In contrast to those elderly purchasers or renters of housing in the private marketplace, low-income elderly persons, or older persons in declining health are more likely to move into government-subsidized or collective or institutional housing. Government-subsidized senior citizen apartments, for example, offer modestly priced rental accommodation for low-income elderly persons who are otherwise able to live independently. Rental prices may be fixed at some reasonable level or are often scaled to ability to pay, for example, 25 percent of gross income. These rental units generally attract local rather than distant movers. They have been popular where available and serve to facilitate local relocation. Mercer (1979) argues that Canadian housing policy has tended to emphasize construction of new accommodation. The federal National Housing Act of 1944 and subsequent related legislation provided a variety of grants and subsidies to enable the construction of new housing. Mercer argues that such housing should be geographically distributed in the same proportion as the distribution of elderly citizens so that elderly persons requiring subsidized housing would have to move only a short distance. Such a policy assumes that the majority of low-income elderly movers prefer to remain within the general area where they currently reside.

Mercer (1979) goes on to suggest that perhaps too much emphasis has been placed on the construction of new housing for low-income elderly persons. He argues that more emphasis is now being placed on programs to assist the elderly to remain in their own houses or apartments. This strategy assumes that many of the low-income elderly prefer to remain where they are, or at least, should be free to make their own choice of location. Various forms of assistance to help the low-income elderly remain in their own homes include forgiveness or reduction of property tax for homeowners, rental assistance grants for renters, grants for home improvement or for adaptation of a house or apartment for wheelchair users, partial rebates for home-heating expenses, and home-care services ranging from visiting nurses and therapists to homemakers, handymen, and meals-on-wheels. The existence of such programs helps the low-income elderly to stay in their present housing or to afford to rent existing housing in the private marketplace. In other words, such programs help to prevent, or at least, forestall, moves into public or institutional housing.

For those elderly persons who are unable to live independently, senior citizen housing offering room, board, and housekeeping is often available. Again, this housing alternative tends to appeal to the local elderly person and, in any case, residence requirements tend to discourage interprovincial migration solely to take advantage of senior citizen housing in another province.

Finally, nursing homes serve those elderly persons who require institutional care including room, board, and a degree of medical surveillance and/or attention. These homes may be privately or publicly owned, for profit or not for profit. In any case, government regulations apply, and provincial governments tend to be involved, alongside private entrepreneurs, in the delivery of nursing home services. Again, these facilities tend to serve local residents whose health dictates a move into an institutional setting.

Immigration Policy

From a policy point of view, the international movement of the world's elderly population is influenced by restrictions on in- and out-migration. Virtually all countries have in-migration restrictions, and some countries restrict emigration. In Canada, the elderly are free to out-migrate to any country that will permit their entry. Elderly residents of other countries may seek entry into Canada subject to current immigration guidelines. Of course, many elderly international movers relocate on a seasonal, rather than permanent, basis and cross the border as visitors rather than as permanent migrants.

Immigration influences population age structure and, consequently, immigration policy may be employed in attempts to influence the age structure of the population. For example, if Canada's elderly were to migrate permanently in large numbers to Florida and Arizona or to France and Italy, then the aging of the Canadian population would be offset. Such an outflow of elderly is unlikely, however, and such outflows, or lacks thereof, are unlikely to become a matter of policy given that Canada does not regulate emigration. On the other side of the coin, Canada does have specific policies regulating in-migration, and the in-migration of the non-elderly, for example, may offset the aging of the population and add to the labour force, increasing its ability to support the non-working elderly population. However, if these non-elderly migrants bring their aged parents to Canada, then again there is pressure on the aging trend. Further, non-elderly migrants (especially persons aged twenty-five to forty) will add to the baby boom population (which at the time of writing comprises persons twenty-five to forty years of age) and contribute to the future geriatric boom that will begin around the year 2011 when the first of the baby boomers turn sixty-five. Of course, continued heavy in-migration of the non-elderly could offset both the population aging trend and the expected geriatric boom. Finally, given that immigrants have preferences for selected locales, for example, the cities of Toronto, Vancouver, and Montreal, and are free to locate wherever they choose, the effects of international in-migration on population age structures will vary within Canada from province to province, city to city, and from rural to urban context.

THE IMPLICATIONS OF GEOGRAPHIC MOBILITY FOR POLICY

The aging of the Canadian population, that is, the increase in the proportion of the population that is aged sixty-five and older, together with the movement of that population, has implications for Canadian public policies (see, for example, McDaniel 1986, 67–92; Myles and Boyd 1983; Stone and Marceau 1977, 51–53; Stone and Fletcher 1980). The aging of the population means that an increasing proportion of the adult population is excluded from the labour force and is supported by a decreasing proportion of non-elderly adult workers. Population aging means that the contribution rates for the Canada Pension Plan will have to rise to more than double their present level (see Health and Welfare Canada 1986b; National Council of Welfare 1982) and that the cost of Old Age Security and its supplementary programs — Guaranteed Income Supplement, Spouse's Allowance, Widowed Spouse's Allowance, et cetera — will also rise (Denton and Spencer 1984). As the costs of supporting a large "retired" population increase, there will be more and more motivation to do away with mandatory retirement and to re-examine the concept of universality wherein all elderly persons, regardless of economic need, receive benefits such as Old Age Security payments (see for example, Myles 1982, 56; 1984, 120). Further, the aging of the population has implications for the delivery and cost of health care services including the training of health care personnel and the building and staffing of health care facilities. Finally, population aging has implications for services such as transportation and housing tailored to the needs and incomes of the elderly.

Hertzman and Hayes (1985) addressed the question, "Will the elderly really bankrupt us with increased health care costs?" That is, as the elderly proportion of the population increases, will future health care costs become excessive? The authors compare two different projections for the years 1976–2026 for the province of Ontario. The first projection originates with Gross and Schwenger (1981) and assumes no change in age- and sex-specific disease rates. The second, more optimistic, projection assumes an extension of average life expectancy and a compression of the period of morbidity preceding death (Fries and Crapo 1981). The Gross and Schwenger projection estimates that the total (constant) dollar cost of health care for the elderly population will triple while the more optimistic projection estimates an increase of only ten percent. Of course, the assumptions on which these projections rest remain hypotheses which may or may not be confirmed as the future unfolds.

Denton and Spencer (1983a; see also 1980, 1983b, and 1986) provided estimates for Canada for 1981–2051 of the possible effects of Canada's changing age structure on overall health care costs. These authors assumed that the per capita cost of health care for a twenty-year-old or for a sixty-year-old, et cetera, will not change, even though the proportion of twenty-year-olds or sixty-year-olds in the population will change. In other words, Denton and Spencer assume that there will not be changes in average health for given ages; that is, they do not assume a compression of morbidity. (Nevertheless, these authors do assume modest increases in life expectancy.) A variety of projections are provided depending on various assumptions about future fertility rates. (For all projections, it is assumed that death rates will decline gradually to the year 2026 and then stabilize, and that in- and out-migration are constant at specified levels.) Under the assumption of relatively low fertility (1.5 births per woman from the year 1991 on), the elderly proportion of the population increases dramatically to almost 27 percent by the year 2051. Per capita health care costs are projected to increase 42 percent and health care as a proportion of the gross national product (GNP) is projected to rise from 7.0 to 9.4 percent. Under high fertility, a radically different picture is obtained. If births were three per woman from the year 1991 on, the elderly proportion of the population would peak at just over 14 percent in the year 2031 and then decline. Per capita health care costs would increase by up to only 10 or 11 percent in the peak years and reach 9.2 percent of GNP (up from the current 7.0 percent). In other words, low fertility exaggerates population aging and increases health care costs, while high fertility offsets population aging and restricts increases in per capita health costs. Nevertheless, while per capita health care costs are lowest under high fertility, because of the large proportion of children that would exist in this scenario, the labour force would be relatively small and therefore, health care as a proportion of GNP would be relatively high. An intermediate level of fertility provides the optimal proportion of GNP committed to health care. Remember that changes in age structure affect not only health care costs, but also influence the relative size of the labour force and therefore the productive capacity of the population (Denton and Spencer 1980, 232; Denton et al. 1986, 86). While per capita health care costs are lowest under high fertility (a relatively high proportion of children and a relatively low proportion of the aged in the population), the relative size of the labour force and therefore the productive capacity of the population is optimal when the total proportion of children and aged persons is relatively small (as is obtained under intermediate levels of fertility). In other words, population change influences not only "demand" for services but also influences the "supply" of services. Denton and Spencer (1983a, 161; also see Denton et al. 1986, 94) conclude that, whether fertility rates and mortality rates go up or down, health care costs will rise, although, even under the worst scenario, *not* to crisis levels.

Messinger and Powell (1987) reach a similar conclusion. These authors examined social spending including the costs of health care, Old Age Security programs, unemployment insurance, education, welfare, and so on. They examined projections (from Statistics Canada) to the year 2031 and concluded that, while demographic changes will be significant, they are unlikely to lead to any serious problem and, in any case, there is plenty of time to anticipate future needs. Under assumptions of 1.66 children per woman, net migration of fifty thousand, and modest increases in life expectancy, Messinger and Powell determine that social spending for all age groups will grow at a faster rate than the population. They conclude that population aging will definitely force social spending upwards, especially during the geriatric boom years of 2011 to 2031. While the percentage of the GNP devoted to all social spending was 21 percent in 1984, the authors note that this percentage will rise, in response to demographic changes alone, from 22 percent in 2001 to almost 30 percent in 2031. In contrast to this "medium-growth" projection, low-growth or high-growth scenarios have quite different implications for future population age composition and social expenditures. However, the *proportion* of GNP devoted to all social expenditures is fairly consistent across the different projections, approaching 30 percent in 2031. Further, the authors speculate that positive economic developments (such as increased worker productivity, technological advance, and lower unemployment) could, according to one optimistic projection, raise the GNP such that projected social expenditures as a proportion of the GNP will actually fall, despite the aging of the population and despite the increased costs of Old Age Security, pensions, and health care programs. After considering a variety of demographic, economic, and other changes that might occur in the next fifty years, Messinger and Powell (1987, 583; see also Foot 1982, 123–44, 215–22) conclude that "the future situation still does not appear to be one of doom and gloom ..."

The geographic mobility of the population can complicate the issues arising from population aging. Without geographic mobility, the population would age in place, "naturally." Without mobility, regional rates of aging would be a function of existing age structures and of local birth and death rates. Migration can complicate the process of population aging by increasing the variability in the concentration of elderly persons in different regions. The out-migration of the non-elderly and/or the in-migration of the elderly exaggerates population aging; the in-migration of the non-elderly and/or the out-migration of the elderly offsets the population aging process. Because the migration of both elderly and non-elderly persons is not random but rather is selective for both origin and destination, migration has the potential for exacerbating regional disparities. In other words, migration can result in concentrations of elderly persons created either by the inflow of elderly migrants or by the outflow of non-elderly migrants (leaving voluntary stayers and trapped, that is, poor and/or otherwise dependent elderly stayers behind). Concentrations of elderly persons — gerontic enclaves (United States Bureau of the Census 1984, 35) — tend to emerge in small towns rather than in rural areas, in certain large cities especially in the central city cores, in some provinces or in selected regions of those provinces, and in congregate housing such as retirement villages and nursing homes.[7] Such concentrations may present special problems for local housing, health care delivery, and so on. These problems often require policy solutions from all levels of government — local, provincial, and federal. The following sections examine the policy implications of long-distance permanent and seasonal migration and of changes of residence occasioned by loss of independence.

The Policy Implications of Long-distance Permanent Migration

Longino and Biggar (1982) examined the impact of elderly United States interstate migrants on service delivery. First of all, these authors note (p. 153) that while rates of elderly interstate migration are about one-half the level of non-elderly interstate movement, nevertheless, elderly migration is more "channelled" than non-elderly migration and may have more serious consequences for service delivery in major receiving and sending states. However, Longino and Biggar (1982, 153) observe that not only is migration selective with respect to origin and destination, it is also selective with respect to who migrates. Long-distance elderly migrants tend to be the younger elderly and therefore healthier, tend to have more education and higher incomes, and are more likely married and less likely widowed. Therefore, in Longino and Biggar's words:

> The implication of these findings is that migration of older people, in the short run at least, probably boosts the local economy without increasing service demand. On the other hand, these findings also imply that migration losses to the major sending states probably do not reduce service demand at all but, rather, concentrate it more in the residual population.

Longino and Biggar (1982, 155–56) go on to argue that a state benefits when it gains younger, healthier elderly persons through in-migration and loses older, more dependent elderly persons through out-migration. On the other hand, when a state receives more older, dependent elders than it loses through out-migration, then the elderly population's demand for services in that state should increase over time as a result. For example, Longino and Biggar (1982, 156–58) suggest that the amenity migration of younger, healthier, and wealthier elderly couples to popular destinations such as Florida or Arizona may be followed in time, as these persons experience widowhood and/or declines in health and/or socio-economic status, by "dependency dominated return migration" wherein many of these increasingly dependent elderly persons return to those states where they spent most of their adult lives and where familiarity, and adult offspring, relatives, and friends may offer degrees of support. Such migration patterns imply that service demands from the elderly population will be most pressing in the "home" state rather that in the "amenity" state. In short, Longino and Biggar emphasize the importance of migration selectivity for service delivery.

Suppose that younger, married, healthier, and wealthier elderly migrants stream from the Prairies to British Columbia or from Eastern Canada to southern Ontario. Both British Columbia and southern Ontario would benefit from an influx of residents who would not compete for jobs or join the ranks of the unemployed. Rather, these new residents would spend money and would create a demand for additional services, thereby creating jobs and otherwise stimulating the local economy. These elderly persons would bring their pensions, their Old Age Security and investment incomes, and perhaps their life savings. They would rent or purchase housing, and spend money on food, clothing, recreation, and so on. The great bulk of these new consumer demands would constitute economic opportunity and benefit for British Columbia and for southern Ontario (and loss for the migrants' home provinces). Demand for medical and hospital services and for government-subsidized housing and institutional residences would increase only modestly at first. In time, these elderly migrants would age and become increasingly at risk of poor health, widowhood, and declining economic circumstances. If these older, increasingly dependent elderly persons stay in British Columbia or southern Ontario, then, in time, pressure is put on local resources. More subsidized housing, more nursing homes, larger health care expenditures, and so on, would be required. At this point, the in-migration of the elderly starts to become a burden rather than a blessing. Of course, if younger, healthier, wealthier, elderly migrants continue to stream into these attractive areas, then the "burden" is offset; that is, the proportion of the elderly population that is dependent remains small, although the absolute number may be large. Alternatively, if substantial proportions of the increasingly older and dependent elderly population migrate back to their provinces of origin, then the "burden" is shifted back to the originating provinces. In short, under these assumptions, the home province loses the benefits of the younger, healthier, wealthier, elderly population but carries the bulk of the burden of caring for the older, more dependent elderly population.

The Policy Implications of Seasonal Migration

Monahan and Greene (1982) examined the impact of the winter season migration of elderly persons to Tucson, Arizona. They note that such seasonal influxes of elderly persons *potentially* have serious implications for access to health care, housing, and social services. Potential problems include (1) high peak-season demand resulting in increased waiting times, decreased quality of services, increased prices, and general "consumer frustration"; and (2) relatively low demand in the off-seasons, with such fluctuations in demand making it difficult to efficiently provide adequate levels of service. Further, there is a perception among both consumers and providers that seasonal migrants contribute substantially to peak loads and compete with permanent residents for services, a competition that permanent residents may resent during the winter season when access to services often becomes limited.

Monahan and Greene tested these allegations and found that the elderly seasonal migrants tended to be younger, healthier (less likely to visit doctor), wealthier, and more likely to be married than were the elderly permanent residents (virtually all of whom were earlier migrants themselves). While increased numbers of elderly persons in the winter season certainly lead to increases in demand, Monahan and Greene (1982, 162) found that:

> ... *patterns* of need and demand for health care resources are not substantially altered by the influx of seasonal migrants, and the changes in *levels* of need and demand are considerably less than the sheer numbers of seasonal migrants might suggest. (Emphasis in the original.)

While emergency room utilization and hospital admissions did rise during the winter season, service capacity did not appear to be strained unduly. Further, the authors concluded that the use of social services such as meals-on-wheels was not extensive for either group and was less for the elderly seasonal migrant than for the elderly permanent resident. Rental housing, however, was found to be in high demand year round, and peak-season demand pushed occupancy rates and rental costs up even further.

Tucker et al. (1987, 13, 16) made similar observations about older Canadians wintering in Florida. These authors observed that the Canadian snowbirds tended to be married, healthy, and reasonably well-off financially, and made little use of health care services and virtually no use at all of social services. Similarily, Monahan and Greene (1982, 163) note that "The picture of the winter visitor that emerges from the data is overwhelmingly one of socially independent individuals whose use of locally subsidized services is slight." While demand for health care is increased during the winter, seasonal migrants and permanent residents have similar use profiles and, consequently, only the level of service and not the service mix is affected. Monahan and Greene conclude that "elderly winter visitors do not create demands on local resources that are significantly to the detriment of the local elderly population." These authors might have also noted that the elderly winter visitors, as consumers of rental housing, food, recreation, and even health care, may provide substantial economic benefits and opportunities for the local community. Indeed, Tucker et al. (1987, 19–20) observe that the Canadian snowbirds that they surveyed in Florida spent US$1,200 per month for an average of five months, paid property tax (three-quarters were property owners), paid sales tax, attracted tourism in the form of visits from family and friends, and made few demands on local social services. As long as elderly visitors pay for services consumed, the local economy benefits — detrimental effects occur only when the local taxpayer is called on to subsidize services, and this seems to rarely happen with seasonal migrants, presumably because hardship either precludes their coming in the first place, or motivates their return home.

Tucker et al. (1987, 9, 15) note that about two-thirds of the respondents to their survey had limited the time that they spent outside of Canada to less than six months in order to remain eligible for Canadian health care insurance. Further, 81 percent had purchased additional private health insurance to supplement their provincial health care coverage. Finally, Tucker et al. (1987, 13, 15, 21) note that while older Canadian seasonal migrants in Florida tend to be among the more healthy, there is the possibility that the Florida life-style is itself health promoting. In any case, seasonal migrants appeared to make less total use of the Canadian health care system.

In addition to the international snowbirds, there may be a "snowbird" phenomenon *within* Canada, although this author is aware of neither anecdotal nor published evidence to that effect. In Canada, many people, elderly and non-elderly alike, spend significant parts of the summer "at the cottage." The winter parallel seems to be the out-of-country vacation, and I am not aware that Canadians, to any significant degree, winter in British Columbia, or southern Ontario, or elsewhere in Canada.

Australia is a country, that, like the United States has population concentrations in both northern and southern regions. Hugo (1986, 26–29) notes that there is evidence of "snowbirding" with elderly residents of the colder, southeastern states wintering in the warmer, northeastern state of Queensland. Hugo suggests that such "bilocality" has implications for shifts in demands for goods and services, and permits "the 'snowbird' to maximize benefits at both origin (maintenance of links with family, friends, and relations) and destination (escaping the cold climate, enjoying the ... recreational resources of a resort area)." Further, Hugo observes that a seasonal migrant may eventually become a permanent migrant. Again, however, it is not at all clear that these Australian patterns are paralleled within Canada.

In any case, snowbirds represent a certain economic loss to the local home economy (pensions and other dollars are spent away from home) and a boom to the receiving economy. Given that the snowbirds tend to be the more independent elderly, the costs to the receiving area in terms of demand for subsidized services is minimal. Further, the snowbirds tend to return home in the event of crisis, putting pressure on services in their home area. In short, the policy implications of seasonal migration are minimal in that the home area continues to provide the bulk of services. Even when the Canadian snowbirds wintering in the United States use American medical services or hospital facilities, reimbursement tends to be sought from the home province's health care plan and tends to be at the local Canadian rates with personal insurance or personal resources making up the difference.

Issues Raised by the Loss of Independence

Independence depends primarily on "health and wealth." Increasing age is associated with increasing risk of loss of either health, wealth, or both, and therefore is associated with an increasing likelihood that one will lose one's independence. The risk of the major causes of mortality — heart disease, cancer, and stroke — increases with age as do the risk of disabling conditions and illnesses ranging from arthritis to Alzheimer's disease. These medical conditions can force a wage earner out of the labour force prematurely and thereby affect income. Further, formal retirement, whether forced or voluntary, also has the effect of reducing monthly income. To make matters worse, the loss of a spouse (often the male because he is older and has a shorter life expectancy) tends to further impoverish the surviving spouse (especially the widow). Indeed, statistics show that the old are more likely to be poor than are the non-elderly, that single persons are more likely to be poor than are those living in a marriage or family circumstance, and that women are more likely to be poor than are men. These risk factors combine in multiple jeopardy fashion such that old and single women (most of whom are widows) are more likely to be poor than any other category, for example, 60 percent of elderly single females as opposed to 25 percent of all elderly persons (National Council of Welfare 1984; see also 1985, 23).

The loss of health, the loss of a spouse, and the loss of income all constrain one's ability to live independently. Nevertheless, the majority of elderly persons do live "independently" either alone or with a spouse (National Council of Welfare 1984, 16). Further, there are various programs, ranging from property tax relief to home care, designed to help elderly persons remain in their own homes. However, the risk of "institutionalization" does rise with age. Recall Table 2.2 (discussed previously in Chapter 2). This table presents data from the 1981 Census of Canada indicating that while less than 2 percent of those persons sixty-five to sixty-nine are institutionalized, more than 35 percent of persons eighty-five and older live in institutional collective dwellings such as hospitals or nursing, chronic care, or old age homes.

Loss of independence, of course, tends to precipitate a change or series of changes of residence. For example, an aging couple might decide to sell their house and move to an apartment. Declining financial resources might lead to a move to a government-subsidized senior citizens' apartment. A stroke suffered by the husband might precipitate his admission to an acute care hospital for a relatively short time, and lead to a longer stay in an extended care hospital, and then perhaps placement in a nursing home. In time, the wife might begin to experience problems associated with heart disease. She might move in with adult offspring for a time, and later enter a senior citizens' lodge. Let me again emphasize that the majority of the elderly population live independently. Nevertheless, the end of life is often preceded by events that lead to changes of residence such that living circumstances are simplified, expenses reduced, and assistance gained either from family or friends or from formal institutional arrangements. Such moves are usually local in nature. Occasionally, an elderly person will move a long distance to live near or with an adult offspring, for example. Such moves are the exception, however, even for those who are independent. In short, loss of independence tends to precipitate changes of residence that are forced and local in nature.

The Experience of Other Countries: Implications for Canada

There are a number of European countries which have much higher proportions of elderly persons than Canada (Population Reference Bureau 1986). Europe is the most "aged" of the continents. In 1986, the elderly age group comprised 13 percent of the population of Europe in comparison to 3 percent in Africa, 4 percent in Asia and Latin America, and 6 percent worldwide. In 1986, Sweden was the most "aged" of nations with 17 percent of its total population being sixty-five and older. Denmark, Norway, West Germany, and the United Kingdom were tied at 15 percent. By comparison, the elderly age group made up 10 percent of the Canadian population and 12 percent of the United States population. Denton and Spencer (1983a, 161; see also Myles 1984, 106; McDaniel 1986, 32–33) point out that countries such as Sweden, West Germany, and the United States already commit the proportions of GNP to health care that are anticipated in Canada near the height of the geriatric boom in the first quarter or third of the twenty-first century. Nevertheless, Sweden, West Germany, the United States and Canada are far from finished with respect to the process of population aging.

Guillemard (1983, 97; see also Myles 1984, 2) observes that "... in industrialized nations today the largest percentage of public expenditure goes to the elderly. The welfare state is, first and foremost, a 'welfare-state-for-the-aged.' " This observation should become increasingly salient as the industrialized nations continue to age well into the twenty-first century. Indeed, various individuals debate the implications of the "graying of the budget" (see, for example, Neugarten 1981, xi). While none of Europe's "aged" nations are currently in crisis with respect to the social costs of population aging, and while this bodes well for Canada as it ages from the current level of 10 percent elderly persons in the population to Europe's current levels of 15 or 17 percent, nevertheless, no nation as a whole (excepting certain regions, such as Florida) has as yet experienced the 20, 25, or perhaps even 30 percent figures that may be reached in the first half of the twenty-first century. If the elderly population continues to be increasingly mobile, and if mobility patterns result in concentrations of elderly persons in selected locales, then whatever problems that might attend the delivery and cost of social services in the twenty-first century may well be compounded in the "gerontic enclaves."

In summary, relatively high concentrations of elderly persons are the result of a number of factors including aging in place (as a result of low fertility and long life expectancy), and out-migration of the non-elderly and/or in-migration of the elderly. Migration patterns both influence and are influenced by policy. For example, regulations requiring that a person retire at a given age free an employee from the labour force and provide the retiree with the option of changing residence. Further, because private pensions and Canada Pension Plan payments are received regardless of place of residence, there is no constraint on mobility other than the purchasing power of those payments. This is also true of the universal Old Age Security benefit;. however, the supplementary benefits are lost if a person leaves Canada for more than six months. In other words, Old Age Security policies do not restrict mobility within Canada but may constrain permanent migration out of Canada, encouraging "snowbirding" instead. Similarly, health care insurance coverage discourages international movement but does not constrain mobility within Canada. Finally, the provision of housing for elderly persons is a factor influencing choice of residence, especially for those elderly persons who are economically or otherwise dependent.

While policy influences migration, it is also true that migration patterns influence policy. Large concentrations of older persons require that policies be adjusted in order to adequately provide services in such areas as housing, social services, and health care. A high proportion of older persons is often viewed as an economic "burden" which depends heavily on publicly funded services. However, from another point of view, the aged population represents a "growth industry." The elderly infuse private capital (private income and savings) and public capital (government transfer payments to individuals and government grants and payments to service industries such as health care and institutional housing) into local economies. Indeed, because of potential economic benefits, it is conceivable that local areas may implement aggressive strategies designed to attract elderly migrants. In short, while migration patterns often require adjustments of public policy, it is also true that policy influences migration patterns.

NOTES

1. It is likely that greater proportions of future cohorts of elderly persons will receive benefits from private pension plans. Employers are increasingly likely to offer a pension program, and survivor benefits are increasingly common.
2. Maximum benefits paid in 1987 to a person age sixty-five were $521.52 monthly or $312.91 monthly to a widowed spouse sixty-five years of age or older ($290.30 if surviving spouse is under sixty-five years of age).
3. As of January 1987, monthly payments for Old Age Security were $297.37. Monthly Guaranteed Income Supplements were $353.41 for a single person and $460.34 for an elderly couple. The Spouse's Allowance was $527.42 monthly and the Widowed Spouse's Allowance was $582.42.
4. See note 3 above.
5. See note 3 above.
6. See note 3 above.
7. A gerontic enclave has a relatively high proportion of older residents. Older persons constitute the great majority of the population of a nursing home or of the Horizon Village retirement communities in Edmonton, for example. A neighbourhood in Victoria composed of 20 or 30 percent elderly persons or a small town in Saskatchewan with 15 or 20 percent elderly residents might also be described as a gerontic enclave.

CHAPTER 7

CONCLUSION

In 1980, Lee concluded his article, *Migration of the Aged*, with these words:

> ... the migration of the elderly has increased with time, and the impetus for the movement has not been spent. It will therefore increase with time, and the migratory streams of the elderly will continue to be diffuse in origin and highly specific in destination. What we have so far witnessed is only the beginning of a movement.

Lee was writing primarily of the United States; however, his words apply potentially to all developed countries. The "mass movement" of older persons that Lee expects may, or may not, materialize in Canada. Nevertheless, future cohorts of older Canadians are likely to be increasingly mobile geographically. Further, older migrants are likely to continue to be highly selective with respect to preferred destinations. These factors, that is, increasing mobility and selectivity of destination, coupled with the increase in the proportion of older persons in the population, suggest that in the future certain locations may experience permanently, or at least seasonally, high concentrations of older persons. These high concentrations of older residents will have important effects on local economies and on local demand for housing, social services, health care, and so on.

This monograph has examined the migration of older persons in Canada, and also in the United States, Britain, France, and Australia; and this final chapter contains a summary and discussion, concluding with a review of unanswered questions.

SUMMARY AND DISCUSSION

The geographic mobility of the older population has been largely ignored until recently for several reasons. First, the elderly have constituted only a relatively small proportion of the total population. Second, the older population is less likely to move than the younger population. Third, migration is often studied as an economically motivated labour-force phenomenon with a focus on non-elderly age groups who are most likely to move for reasons of employment and economics. It is a myth, however, that the older population is geographically stationary. The elderly do move, and in signif-

icant numbers. Further, it is a mistake to assume that elderly movers constitute a homogeneous category, moving for similar reasons to similar
destinations. The elderly are a heterogeneous group who move (or stay) for
a wide variety of reasons and who exhibit a number of different movement
patterns.

This monograph focuses on the population fifty-five years of age and
older. In order to assess variability across the later years, this monograph
focuses on the near elderly fifty-five to sixty-four years of age, on the
younger elderly sixty-five to seventy-four years of age, and on the older
elderly seventy-five and more years of age. These are, admittedly, gross
categories, and it is recognized that there is considerable diversity within
any given age group.

It is important to study geographic mobility across the life span, and it is
important to take into account the unique circumstances surrounding each
mover's decision to relocate and the choice of destination. Nevertheless,
certain patterns do emerge, and the focus of this monograph is on those
broad patterns that characterize the mobility of various segments of the
Canadian population: younger and older elderly persons, married and not
married, rich and poor, eastern and western Canadians, French-speaking
and English-speaking persons, and so on. Further, this monograph focuses
not only on who moves and why, but also on who moves where. The first
question focuses on the determinants and probability of movement. The
second question focuses on the consequences of geographic mobility for the
sending and receiving areas. It is possible that, while individuals may be
highly mobile, the number and characteristics of persons leaving an area
may be balanced by a stream of similar persons coming into that area. In
other words, while there is considerable movement of individuals, the character of the population of a given region may remain relatively constant.
Further, it must be stressed that the great majority of moves undertaken by
the elderly are of short rather than long distance. Nevertheless, the long-
distance migration of the older population tends to be "diffuse in origin"
and "highly specific in destination" (Lee 1980, 135). For example, older persons from all over the Prairie Provinces have a tendency to migrate to
south-central and southwestern British Columbia. In other words, the
migration of older persons has a tendency to lead to their concentrations in
selected locations. This "graying" of local or regional populations implies
both social and economic transformations, and there is a tendency to view
these changes with alarm. Again, stereotypes mislead. The stereotypes
make one assume that there will be a sizeable aged population largely composed of frail elderly persons dependent on the non-elderly population for
subsidized housing, social services, health care, and institutional accommodation. While the older population is more likely than the younger population to have such needs, nevertheless, the majority of older persons live
independently and contribute to the local economy and to society. Indeed,

as many entrepreneurs are beginning to discover, the older population is a "growth industry."

Inasmuch as the older population has economic means and needs, it constitutes a significant market. All elderly persons in Canada receive Old Age Security. The poorer elderly receive various income supplements. Many older persons receive income from private pensions and/or from the Canada Pension Plan. Others have personal savings and income sources. In short, the elderly have money to spend on housing, on food and clothing, on recreation, on travel, and so on. At the same time, the older population does not compete with the non-elderly for jobs or strain the unemployment rolls. Local economies can benefit from the influx of older persons. Even when older persons suffer a decline in health and increased dependency, the medical care, hospital, and nursing home industries all benefit as does the local economy through the infusion of provincial and federal health care dollars.

Just as it is important not to stereotype the older population, it is also important not to assume that all older migrants move as a homogeneous group to the same destinations for the same reasons. It is not true, for example, that all interprovincial elderly migrants go to British Columbia. Many do, but certainly not all. Even moves to British Columbia may be variously motivated. Not all older migrants move to British Columbia solely for the advantages of the climate. Some may move to follow adult offspring and grandchildren who have settled there. Others may be returning home after retirement from employment which has taken them to other parts of the country. In short, the geographic mobility of the older population comprises a variety of different kinds of moves.

Most moves are of short distance involving relocation within a local area. Even these moves are far from homogeneous. An independent older person may choose to relocate to a suburb or to an outlying urban area, or may choose to move from a house to an apartment. The poorer elderly in the central city tend to move within the inner city from one inexpensive rental unit to another. Elderly persons who become dependent for reasons of declining health may be "forced" to move into the homes of kin or into institutional accommodation such as senior citizen or nursing homes.

Moves that cross municipal boundaries are referred to as migration as opposed to local mobility. Migration may be within Canada (internal migration) and may be within the province (intraprovincial) or between provinces (interprovincial). Migration may also be between countries (international migration). As with local moves, these longer-distance moves tend to be diverse in character. The independent older person may migrate a considerable distance for a variety of reasons. The older migrant may be moving to some attractive location in order to enjoy an anticipated lifestyle. Alternatively, the older migrant may be returning "home" or moving to live near, or with, an adult offspring. Further, these long-distance moves may be precipitated by the event of retirement, may anticipate retirement (preretirement move), or may follow retirement by some years. Long-distance moves may be voluntary (as in the move to some amenity area for life-style reasons) or may be involuntary, forced by circumstances of declining health and/or economic means. Note that long-distance moves to be near adult offspring or to return home may be voluntary moves made by independent, older persons, or may be relatively forced moves made by increasingly dependent persons seeking support from family and/or community. Finally, migration may be either permanent or temporary. The temporary (seasonal) migration of the older population may be as significant as the patterns of permanent migration; however, seasonal migration patterns are currently not very well documented.

In summary, the geographic mobility of the older population is a multi-faceted phenomenon varying along four dimensions: the degree of permanence (permanent, seasonal), the distance of the move (local, non-local), the motivation for the move (whether voluntary and preference-dominated or forced), and the type of move (retirement, amenity, return, kinship, suburbanization, apartmentalization, institutionalization, et cetera).

Not only are there different patterns of mobility, there are also different types of older movers. That is, the decision to move (or stay), and the choice of destination are influenced by the characteristics of the individual older person. The decision to move is influenced by the older person's assessment of current and potential residence, and of needs, preferences, and resources. There are many reasons to stay in one's current residence (inertial factors) including sentimental attachment, familiarity, and presence of friends and kin. Reasons to move may include locational push factors, such as a cold climate and the deterioration of housing and neighbourhood (environmental stressors), and pull factors, such as a mild climate, a better life-style, a less expensive standard of living, or the distant presence of family or friends. The decision to move may be triggered by personal events such as retirement, children leaving home, death of a spouse, loss of health, or loss of economic independence. Further, the decision to move and the choice of destination are tempered by experiential and tangible resources including one's experience with past mobility and with the potential destination, and one's economic and health statuses. Finally, distance tends to deter movement, and the probability of a move to a given place tends to decrease with increasing distance. Just the same, the probability of long-distance moves appears to be increasing in recent decades and may continue to increase in the future.

Geographic mobility is often viewed largely as an economic phenomenon, with people moving primarily for reasons of employment and/or standard of living. The employment factor is largely irrelevant to elderly mobility, although other economic variables including income, cost of living, and cost of relocation all remain salient. Alternatively, mobility is often viewed simply as a demographic phenomenon characterized by flows of persons from one place to another. This demographic approach tends to examine the objective characteristics of movers including age, sex, socio-economic status, marital status, ethnicity, and so on. While there is a great deal of data on such variables (primarily from the quinquennial Censuses), this monograph is committed to a socio-demographic explanation of mobility (see Lee 1966; Wiseman 1980). That is, it is argued that geographic mobility has to be explained not only in terms of the objective characteristics of various population subgroups and of various locations, but also in terms of the subjective characteristics (attitudes, values, beliefs, perceptions, et cetera) of individuals. However, such subjective data are not collected in the Census, and social surveys exploring the geographic mobility of older Canadians are, at the time of writing, very rare.

This monograph has reviewed existing literature on the geographic mobility of older Canadians, and has presented an analysis of 1981 Census data (for the 1976 to 1981 period) and of Old Age Security data (for the 1971 to 1985 period). The findings indicate, on the one hand, that the elderly are highly stable residentially, with over one-half of aged persons having lived in their current residence for over ten years. On the other hand, the elderly do move and are increasingly likely to move from one province to another. Nevertheless, most moves are local in nature, covering relatively short distances. Older females (many of whom are widowed) are more likely than older males to make shorter-distance moves; however, older males (many of whom are married and older than their spouse) are more likely than older females to move long distances. Just the same, married older persons are less mobile generally than the never married and widowed; the divorced and separated are the most mobile. The better educated, especially the university educated, having been more mobile generally throughout their lives and having greater financial means, are most likely to move long distances; the less educated are more likely to move locally. Older persons of higher socio-economic status, having been able to afford comfortable housing earlier in their working life, are less likely to move locally; however, after retirement, the economically advantaged are more likely to make preference-dominated long-distance moves. Finally, Francophones, most of whom reside in the province of Quebec, are less likely than Anglophones to move from one province to another.

The 1981 Census data provide evidence for different kinds of moves. For example, older persons not resident in the province of their birth are more likely to migrate interprovincially than are older persons residing in their home province. This pattern suggests a certain degree of return migration as persons migrate back to their province of origin. There is also some evidence for a retirement-age peak in migration patterns suggesting that the event of retirement may trigger residential mobility. Further, the heavy flow of retirees into British Columbia, for example, suggests that retirement migration motivated by the pull of amenities and the promise of an improved quality of life is a significant phenomenon in Canada.

The migration of the elderly and non-eldery populations is resulting, to a degree, in the graying of certain areas of Canada. However, given that the elderly and non-elderly tend to have similar origins and destinations, at the provincial level at least, the movement of the elderly tends to be offset by the movement of the non-elderly. Nevertheless, concentrations of older persons do result through either the out-migration of the non-elderly or the in-migration of the elderly. For example, while the elderly often leave Saskatchewan, because of the even heavier out-migration of the non-elderly, the province has a high concentration of older persons who have been "left behind." In contrast, heavy in-migration of older persons has given the city of Victoria a very high proportion of older residents.

Mobility patterns vary across Canada, tending to be low in the Atlantic Provinces and high in the West, especially in Alberta and British Columbia. Mobility tends to be high in cities such as Montreal, Calgary, Edmonton, Vancouver, and Victoria. Victoria and Calgary are popular destinations for older migrants from out-of-province. Montreal's high rate of elderly mobility, on the other hand, is a function of the movement of its local population, and few older persons move to Montreal from out-of-province. At the provincial level, British Columbia, Ontario, and Alberta are popular destinations for older out-of-province migrants. In contrast, Quebec is seldom chosen as a destination by non-Quebecers.

The migration of the elderly in Canada is predominantly westward. Ontario has significant net gains of older persons, many coming from Quebec. British Columbia gains more older residents through migration than any other province, many of these migrants coming from the Prairie Provinces and Ontario.

Several of Canada's largest cities lose more older residents than they gain. Montreal, Toronto, Winnipeg, Edmonton, and — despite its being a frequently chosen destination — Vancouver, all have net losses of older residents due to migration. Victoria, to a greater degree than any other major city, gains more older persons than it loses through migration. In southern Ontario, cities such and St. Catharines-Niagara, Kitchener, and London are net gainers. The general pattern, however, for Canada's major cities, is a net out-migration of the aged population. Nevertheless, the majority of Canada's older population continues to reside in the larger urban centres.

The tendency to move varies with age and with position in the life cycle. Young adults are, by far, the most mobile age group. Nevertheless, the older population does move with significant frequency. There is some evidence that migration propensity increases near the time of retirement as persons make voluntary, preference-dominated moves. Mobility may also increase near the end of life as forced moves become more likely.

Canada's patterns of aged mobility are similar to those of other developed nations. Canada's closest neighbour, the United States, also has net out-migration from the larger cities, and a significant interstate flow from the Snowbelt to the Sunbelt in the South and Southwest. Interstate migrants in the United States, as in Canada, tend to be the younger, married, healthier, and wealthier elderly. There is evidence of a significant volume of retirement-motivated migration, perhaps to a greater extent than in Canada, and of return migration patterns. These migration patterns are resulting in the graying of popular destination areas such as Florida and Arizona. Seasonal "snowbird" migration is also a significant American pattern, and not a small percentage of these snowbirds wintering in the American Sunbelt are older Canadians. Unlike the United States, Canada does not have a large seasonal elderly population moving within Canada. Neither does Canada have huge retirement communities such as Sun City and Sun City West in Arizona, although such developments may yet take place.

Britain also has a significant retirement migration phenomenon involving movement to popular coastal resort towns. As in Canada and the United States, Britain's elderly are increasingly likely to migrate and increasingly likely to move longer distances. Migration patterns in both Britain and the United States have produced concentrations of older persons in certain areas that are far in excess of Canada's highest concentrations. While these "gray," gerontic enclaves transform the social and economic landscape, crises in housing, social services, health care, and so on, are notably absent. The experience of the United Kingdom and the United States suggests that Canada will be able to accommodate significantly increased concentrations of aged persons both generally and in selected locales.

Australia, like Canada, the United States, and Britain, has a pattern of increasing retirement migration involving movement to coastal and sunnier climates. There is also some evidence of patterns of two-home ownership and seasonal migration.

Migration patterns in France differ somewhat from those in the United States, Britain, and Australia. France has a significant pattern of retirement migration involving the elderly from the largest cities returning to their rural and small town origins. This movement seems to be largely motivated by the high cost of living in the cities and the lower cost of living in the more rural areas; indeed, it is the less wealthy elderly who make these moves. The above migration pattern in France seems unlikely in Canada. Canada's larger cities seem to exert less of a "push" than do the larger cities in France, Britain, and the United States. Just the same, Canada's older population is not gravitating to the larger cities, and may in the future avoid or leave the central metropolitan areas in increasing numbers.

A frequently expressed concern in the developed countries is that population aging coupled with elderly migration will create high concentrations of older persons that will overwhelm local services. Other countries have already survived concentrations in selected areas up to twice as high as Canada's most notable gerontic enclave, Victoria. Further, projected estimates of the future size of Canada's elderly population, coupled with projected estimates of the future size of the labour force, suggest that forthcoming demands will not overly tax the productive capacity of the population. Certainly, policy shifts will be required as the aged population forms an increasingly larger proportion of the population. Resources will have to be shifted from those age groups declining in relative number (for example, the young) to the growing, older age categories. Further, migration involving long-distance relocation may come to be viewed as beneficial to local economies because of the infusion of private and public capital that will accompany the in-migrants. In other words, while there is a tendency to view in-migration as putting pressure on local services, alternatively, such pressure can be viewed positively as promoting economic growth. We might see local chambers of commerce and departments of tourism promoting their areas in attempts to attract elderly migrants. Similarly, seasonal in-migrants tend to benefit local economies. Indeed, the gain of the receiving areas will in part be the loss of the sending areas, especially, given evidence that when problems surface, seasonal migrants tend to return home.

Just as elderly migration and population aging have implications for public policy, so also does policy influence migration. Generally, Canada's Old Age Security and health care provisions, being completely portable, have little, if any, impact on movement within Canada. On the other hand, residency requirements for institutional accommodation may restrict interprovincial movement to a degree. While pensions and the basic Old Age Security payment are portable outside of Canada, health care insurance and supplementary Old Age Security benefits are payable for only the first six months after a person has left Canada. Consequently, these regulations discourage permanent migration out of Canada and, alternatively, encourage seasonal migration.

While much is known about the geographic mobility of the older population, many questions remain to be answered. This monograph concludes with a discussion of unanswered questions.

DIRECTIONS FOR FUTURE RESEARCH

Research on the geographic mobility of the elderly is relatively new. Much remains to be done. On the one hand, there is a need to extend the theoretical explanations and models of elderly mobility (see Wiseman 1980 for an excellent beginning). On the other hand, there is a need for additional empirical research. Many of the empirical studies to date are analyses of census data or of address changes recorded in Old Age Security or income tax files. While these data sources are readily accessible and provide information on a great number of people, they provide information on only a limited number of variables. More social surveys are needed. These surveys should be designed to explore mobility in depth and should focus on demo-graphic, sociological, social-psychological, and economic dimensions. Cost constraints and logistics will tend to limit such surveys to local areas or to selected populations; nevertheless, a number of in-depth surveys conducted in a variety of locales in Canada would add greatly to our understanding of the phenomenon of aged mobility. In order to more fully understand the decision to move or to stay, and the effect of moving or staying on personal well-being, satisfaction, quality of life, and so on, there is a need for more qualitative analyses (for example, case studies, autobiographies, participant observation). Further, in order to more fully understand the process of elderly geographic mobility, there is a need for more comparative (cross-cultural) and historical research. Finally, it is important to move ahead from the fairly straightforward cross-tabular analyses (such as in Chapter 3 of this monograph) to exploration of multivariate models (for example, see the recent — 1985 and 1986 — work of Liaw at McMaster University and of Ledent at the University of Quebec, and their colleagues).

Following is a listing of questions that might specifically be addressed by future research:

1. Given that the majority of the elderly have lived in their present residence for a number of years, that is, given that residential sta-bility is more prominent than residential mobility, there is a need to study stayers as well as movers. What proportion of non-movers stay because they are happy where they are? What pro-portion of non-movers have considered a move, or would like to relocate, but do not, and for what reasons?

2. With respect to mobility motivated by the event of retirement, there is a need to examine separately the decisions to move (or stay) of "early" retirees, retirees at the "normal" age, and "late" retirees. Liaw and Nagnur (1985, 100) conclude that their research "leaves open the question of whether a normal retirement peak in migration exists in most metropolitan areas in Canada." We need to learn more about the effects of retirement on the tendency to move and on who is motivated to move where and for what rea-son. The poorer retiree may move to reduce living costs. The wealthier retiree may move a longer distance to some desirable place, or not move at all, preferring seasonal vacations instead.

3. Not all retirees are healthy and able to make moves of preference. Indeed, retirement itself and associated mobility may both be pre-cipitated by health crises. The extent of poor health in determin-ing mobility is little known. Most of the available data exclude the institutionalized population. We need to know the probability of an older person eventually being institutionalized, and at what age institutionalization is likely to occur. Further, specific studies

are needed of persons in poor health. Very often declining health precipitates a series of moves. It is important to understand the sequencing and timing of these moves, as well as their determinants. For example, a stroke may lead to hospitalization and early retirement. Partial recovery may allow a return to relatively independent living, and the stroke victim and his or her spouse might make a "retirement" move to an amenity area. A second stroke may lead to hospitalization again, and, later, to placement in a nursing home. "Return" migration might follow as the stroke victim and his or her spouse return to their home area to regain familiar surroundings and to obtain the support of family and friends (assistance-motivated "kinship" migration). The stroke victim might be placed in a nursing home, and the spouse might live with an adult offspring pending entrance into a senior citizen lodge. Little is known, empirically, about such mobility patterns, and future research needs to document typical patterns and their occurrence, determinants, and consequences at both the micro (individual) and macro (societal) levels. Further, there is a need to study separately the effects of short-distance moves into nearby institutions and of longer-distance moves into more distant institutions (for example, involving the movement of rural elderly persons into an institution in the city, or of elderly persons to an institution in a different city or province in order to be close to kin).

4. We need to be able to distinguish the different kinds of migration patterns. Though often able to document a person's move from Ontario to British Columbia, we seldom know if the move is a preference-dominated retirement move, a return migration, or a kinship migration motivated by preference or for assistance. Similarly, information is required about the patterns of local mobility. Further, if we could identify the different types of moves, we could also determine their frequency; that is, we could determine how many persons move to be near kin, or to live with kin, or to return home, and so on.

5. To what extent does the cost of living at the place of residence influence the decision to move or stay? Further, to what extent does the cost of living at various possible destinations influence the choice of destination? In other words, do older people flee from, or avoid, expensive locales, and do they move to, or stay, in inexpensive locations? The answer will not be straightforward, but will depend on a number of other variables besides cost of living, including the socio-economic status of the older person and the general attractiveness of the area under consideration. To make this point, it is not at all clear that economically depressed

areas, despite potentially low costs of living, are intrinsically attractive to older Canadians. Pursuing this line of questioning further, to what extent do differentials in provincial benefits and local services influence the relocation of the older population? For example, does Alberta's relatively generous supplement of the federal Guaranteed Income Supplement (given to less wealthy elderly persons) attract the less wealthy elderly from other provinces? Do elderly persons in one location know about or ask about costs of living, governmental benefits, and service costs and availability in other locations? How much of this kind of information is obtained, and how accurate and how influential is it? Are senior citizens' apartments, lodges, and nursing homes perceived to be better, more available, or cheaper in certain locations; and do such perceptions influence relocation patterns? To what extent is it true that the elderly cannot afford to live in larger cities such as Toronto, Calgary, or Vancouver?

6. Simmons (1980, 161) notes that large urban centres have become relatively less attractive to migrants of all ages. He notes that: "A nationwide shift in preference towards smaller places has taken place, although the reasons are still not clear." More needs to be known about the "rural-urban turnaround" and the extent of involvement of older Canadians? Is elderly migration increasingly drawn to the rural fringes of large cities, or to small towns, or to rural areas? Given that the less urban areas are often less advantaged economically, it follows that we need to know whether or not elderly Canadians are increasingly influenced by non-economic, quality-of-life considerations in deciding whether or not, and where, to move.

7. Many older Canadians pursue quality of life through seasonal rather than permanent migration. Marshall, at the University of Toronto, and his colleagues (Marshall and Longino 1987; Tucker et al. 1987), are currently studying Canadian snowbirds in Florida; little, however, is presently known about the extent or nature of the Canadian snowbird phenomenon. How many older Canadians winter in the American Sunbelt? How long do they stay? Who goes where, and with what consequences? Further, is there a seasonal snowbird migration *within* Canada, to British Columbia, southern Ontario, or Prince Edward Island, for example? Is there a parallel pattern of temporary migration in the summer, involving movement to coastal areas, mountains, lakes, and so on? Do these movements involve significant numbers of the elderly? How many are travelling long distances? What are the implications for local economies and for local service delivery? How many older Canadians own second homes? Indeed, how

many *non-elderly* Canadians own second homes in winter or summer vacationlands or own motor homes? Such practices among today's non-elderly may influence future elderly mobility patterns as the non-elderly age.

8. While we know a great deal about geographic mobility in and between provinces, or in the larger cities, because census data are not identifiable for smaller jurisdictions (to preserve confidentiality), little is known about migration patterns in smaller towns and villages, and in rural areas. We know a lot about migration to Victoria, but little, if anything, about migration to Vancouver Island, or to the Okanagan Valley.

9. We know little about the international migration of the elderly. How many older Canadians leave Canada permanently? Who are they? Why do they leave? Where do they go? Is this an increasingly common occurence? Further, we know that there is not insubstantial migration of older persons into Canada. Who are these migrants? Are some returning ex-Canadians? Are some the parents of recent migrants to Canada? Where do these older migrants come from? Why do they come to Canada?

10. There is a need for more cohort analyses. That is, we need to identify individuals born about the same time, and we need to follow these people across their life spans to assess the probabilities of various kinds of moves over the life course. The analysis presented in Chapter 3 is largely cross-sectional (that is, it studies people born at different points in time) and fails to separate the effects of social change and of aging per se. In other words, we need studies that attempt to separate the age, cohort, and period effects on mobility patterns; that is, that separate the effects of a person's getting older, the cumulative effects of history and of broad social change, and the effects of current events. Along this line of questioning, it is important to distinguish three groups of movers (and non-movers): those who move frequently, those who move rarely, and those who are stationary. Further, it is probable that some individuals will change from one mobility category to another over the course of their lives. For example, some who have been stationary for a long period of time may make a retirement move, or towards the end of life may make a series of forced moves. On the other hand, a lifetime chronic mover may enter a nursing home, for example, and begin a relatively long period of stationary residence. It is important to document the different patterns, their frequencies, their determinants, and their consequences for individuals and for society.

11. Many mobility studies focus either on the individual or on some large aggregate unit such as the city or the province. It is impor-

tant to remember that many older persons are married and move as a couple or as a family when children are present in the home. In addition to focusing on the individual mover, it is also important to examine mobility using the family as the unit of analysis.

12. Finally, it is important to examine the policy and economic implications of the geographic mobility of the older population. As the proportion of older persons in the population increases, and as the older population becomes increasingly mobile and increasingly selective in the choice of destination, it is increasingly likely that there will be significant concentrations of older persons in the future in certain locations. It is important to both the public and the private sectors to anticipate these developments and to anticipate future problems and benefits. We need to plan for the future, and adjust policy as required. Private business needs to estimate the future size of its markets and needs to understand the desires and motivations of the elderly with respect to consumer behaviour. Similarly, the public sector needs to estimate the future demand for public services.

These various questions are important for both academic and practical reasons. As academics, these questions titillate us simply because they are there. An academic's raison d'être is the identification of unanswered questions and the enterprise of providing answers. In other words, the pursuit of knowledge for itself is sufficient justification. On the other hand, mobility/migration involves the movement of real individuals and has consequences, potentially both good and bad, for people's quality of life. Further, mobility/migration has implications, both good and problematic, for the larger society. It is important to anticipate problems and to find humane and practical solutions. It is hoped that our society will continue to allow and even encourage geographic mobility so that individuals can freely make choices that are to their best personal advantage. It is further hoped, that when mobility is forced by unfortunate circumstances (economic, health or otherwise), humane and practical alternatives will continue to be, and will increasingly be, available. Where geographic concentrations of older persons result from the aging of the population and from the migration patterns of both old and young, it is hoped that both the elderly and the communities in which they reside will benefit mutually, and that problems of adequate service delivery will be easily overcome to the benefit of all. The elderly population is too often viewed as a burden; it may be better viewed as an opportunity. If our society responds to the opportunity, the future lives of all Canadians will be enriched.

BIBLIOGRAPHY

Biggar, J. C.
  1980   "Who Moved Among the Elderly, 1965 to 1970." *Research on Aging*
          2:73–91.
Biggar, J. C., C. F. Longino, Jr., and C. B. Flynn
  1980   "Elderly Interstate Migration: Impact on Sending and Receiving States,
          1965 to 1970." *Research on Aging* 2:217–32.
Bryant, E. S., and M. El-Attar
  1984   "Migration and Redistribution of the Elderly: A Challenge to Com-
          munity Services." *The Gerontologist* 24:634–40.
Census of Canada
  1981   *The 1981 Census of Canada*. Catalogue Number 92–901.
Cheung, H. Y., and K. Liaw
  1986   *Metropolitan Outmigration of Elderly Females in Canada: Char-
          acterization and Explanation*. QSEP Research Report No. 182.
          Hamilton: McMaster University (Program for Quantitative Studies in
          Economics and Population, Faculty of Social Sciences).
Chevan, A., and L. R. Fischer
  1979   "Retirement and Interstate Migration." *Social Forces* 57:1365–80.
Connidis, I.
  1983   "Living Arrangement Choices of Older Residents: Assessing Quan-
          titative Results with Qualitative Data." *Canadian Journal of Sociology*
          8:359–75.
Courchene, T. J.
  1970   "Interprovincial Migration and Economic Adjustment." *Canadian Jour-
          nal of Economics* 3:550–76.
  1974   *Migration, Income, and Employment: Canada, 1965–68*. Montreal:
          C. D. Howe Research Institute.
Cribier, F.
  1975   "Retirement Migration in France." In L. A. Kosinski and R. M. Prothero
          (eds.), *People on the Move: Studies on Internal Migration*. London:
          Methuen.
  1980   "A European Assessment of Aged Migration." *Research on Aging*
          2:255–70.
Denton, F. T., C. H. Feaver, and B. G. Spencer
  1986   "Prospective Aging of the Population and its Implications for the
          Labour Force and Government Expenditures." *Canadian Journal on
          Aging* 5:75–98.
Denton, F. T. and B. G. Spencer
  1980   "Health-Care Costs when the Population Changes." In V. W. Marshall
          (ed.), *Aging in Canada*. Don Mills: Fitzhenry and Whiteside.

1983a "Population Aging and Future Health Costs in Canada." *Canadian Public Policy* IX:155–63.

1983b *The Sensitivity of Health-Care Costs to Changes in Population Age Structure.* QSEP Research Report No. 74. Hamilton: McMaster University (Program for Quantitative Studies in Economics and Population, Faculty of Social Sciences).

1984 *Prospective Changes in the Population and Their Implications for Government Expenditures.* QSEP Research Report No. 98. Hamilton: McMaster University (Program for Quantitative Studies in Economics and Population, Faculty of Social Sciences).

Flynn, C. B., C. F. Longino, Jr., R. F. Wiseman, and J. C. Biggar
1985 "The Redistribution of America's Older Population: Major National Migration Patterns for Three Census Decades, 1960–1980." *The Gerontologist* 25:292–96.

Foot, D. K.
1982 *Canada's Population Outlook: Demographic Futures and Economic Challenges.* Toronto: Lorimer and Canadian Institute for Economic Policy.

Frey, W. H.
1984 "Lifecourse Migration of Metropolitan Whites and Blacks and the Structure of Demographic Change in Large Central Cities." *American Sociological Review* 49:803–27.

1986 "Lifecourse Migration and Redistribution of the Elderly Across U.S. Regions and Metropolitan Areas." *Economic Outlook USA* 13:10–16.

Fries, J. F.
1983 "The Compression of Morbidity." *Milbank Memorial Fund Quarterly/Health and Society* 61:397–419.

Fries, J. F., and L. M. Crapo
1981 *Vitality and Aging.* San Francisco: W. H. Freeman.

George, M. V.
1970 *Internal Migration in Canada: Demographic Analyses.* Ottawa: Dominion Bureau of Statistics, Queen's Printer.

Gober, P., and L. E. Zonn
1983 "Kin and Elderly Amenity Migration." *The Gerontologist* 23:288–94.

Golant, S. M.
1972 *The Residential Location and Spatial Behavior of the Elderly: A Canadian Example.* Research Paper No. 143. Chicago: Department of Geography, University of Chicago.

Goldscheider, C.
1971 *Population, Modernization, and Social Structure.* Boston: Little, Brown.

Grant, E. K., and A. E. Joseph
1983 "The Spatial Aspects and Regularities of Multiple Interregional Migration within Canada: Evidence and Implications." *The Canadian Journal of Regional Science* 6:75–96.

Grant, E. K., and J. Vanderkamp
1976 *The Economic Causes and Effects of Migration: Canada 1965–71.* Economic Council of Canada. Ottawa: Supply and Services Canada.

1984 "A Descriptive Analysis of the Incidence and Nature of Repeat Migration Within Canada, 1968–71." *Canadian Studies in Population* 11:61–77.

1986 "Repeat Migration and Disappointment." *Canadian Journal of Regional Science* 9:299–322.

Gross, M. J., and C. W. Schwenger

1981 *Health Care Costs for the Elderly in Ontario: 1976–2026.* Toronto: Ontario Economic Council.

Guillemard, A.

1983 "The Making of Old Age Policy in France." In A. Guillemard (ed.), *Old Age and the Welfare State*. Beverly Hills: Sage.

Health and Welfare Canada

1984 *Chronology of Selected Social Welfare Legislation by Program: 1876–1983.* Ottawa.

1986a *Medical Care Annual Report 1983–4.* Ottawa: Minister of Supply and Services Canada.

1986b *The Canada Pension Plan: Financing the Canada Pension Plan.* News release.

Heaton, T. B., W. B. Clifford, and G. V. Fuguitt

1980 "Changing Patterns of Retirement Migration: Movement Between Metropolitan and Nonmetropolitan Areas." *Research on Aging* 2:93–104.

1981 "Temporal Shifts in the Determinants of Young and Elderly Migration in Nonmetropolitan Areas." *Social Forces* 60:4–60.

Heintz, K. M.

1976 *Retirement Communities: For Adults Only.* New Brunswick, New Jersey: Center for Urban Policy Research.

Henretta, J. C.

1986 "Retirement and Residential Moves by Elderly Households." *Research on Aging* 8:23–37.

Hertzman, C., and M. Hayes

1985 "Will the Elderly Really Bankrupt Us With Increased Health Care Costs?" *Canadian Journal of Public Health* 76:373–77.

Hogan, T. D.

1987 "Determinants of the Seasonal Migration of the Elderly to Sunbelt States." *Research on Aging* 9:115–33.

Hoyt, G. C.

1954 "The Life of the Retired in a Trailer Park." *American Journal of Sociology* 19:361–70.

Hugo, G.

1986 *Population Aging in Australia: Implications for Social and Economic Policy.* Papers of the East-West Population Institute, No. 98. Honolulu: East-West Center.

Kalbach, W. E.

1970 *The Impact of Immigration on Canada's Population.* Ottawa: Dominion Bureau of Statistics, Queen's Printer.

Kim, J., and G. Hartwigsen
  1983 "The Current Population Shift Among Elderly Migrants." *Research on Aging* 5:269-82.
Kosinski, L. A.
  1976 "How Population Movement Reshapes the Nation." *Canadian Geographical Journal* 92:34-39.
Krout, J. A.
  1983 "Seasonal Migration of the Elderly." *The Gerontologist* 23:295-99.
La Gory, M., R. Ward, and T. Juravich
  1980 "The Age Segregation Process: Explanation for American Cities." *Urban Affairs Quarterly* 16:59-80.
Law, C. M., and A. M. Warnes
  1973 "The Movement of Retired People to Seaside Resorts: A Study of Morecambe and Llandudno." *Town Planning Review* 44:373-90.
Ledent, J., and K. Liaw
  1986 *Characteristics, Causes, and Consequences of Elderly Migration in Canada, 1976-1981: An Analysis Based on Micro Data.* Montreal: Institut national de la rechérche scientifique, Université du Québec. Also released as QSEP Research Report No. 184. Hamilton: McMaster University (Program for Quantitative Studies in Economics and Population, Faculty of Social Sciences).
Lee, E. S.
  1966 "A Theory of Migration." *Demography* 3:47-57.
  1980 "Migration of the Aged." *Research on Aging* 2:131-35.
Lemon, A.
  1973 "Retirement and its Effect on Small Towns: The Example of Norfolk and Suffolk." *Town Planning Review* 44:254-62.
Liaw, K., and P. Kanaroglou
  1985 *Metropolitan Outmigration Pattern of the Elderly in Canada: 1971-76.* QSEP Research Report No. 124. Hamilton: McMaster University (Program for Quantitative Studies in Economics and Population, Faculty of Social Sciences). Also in *Research on Aging* 8(1986):201-31.
Liaw, K., and D. N. Nagnur
  1985 "Characterization of Metropolitan and Nonmetropolitan Outmigration Schedules of the Canadian Population System, 1971-1976." *Canadian Studies in Population* 12:81-102.
Longino, C. F., Jr., and J. C. Biggar
  1981 "The Impact of Retirement Migration on the South." *The Gerontologist* 21:283-90.
  1982 "The Impact of Population Redistribution on Service Delivery." *The Gerontologist* 22:153-59.
Lycan, R.
  1969 "Interprovincial Migration in Canada: The Role of Spatial and Economic Factors." *Canadian Geographer* 13:237-54.
Marr, W. L., D. J. McCready, and F. W. Millerd
  1977 "Canadian Resource Reallocation: Interprovincial Labour Migration, 1966-1971." *Canadian Studies in Population* 4:17-31.
  1978 "Canadian Interprovincial Migration and Education, 1966-1971." *Canadian Studies in Population* 5:1-11.

Marshall, V. W., and C. F. Longino
1987 "The Networks of Seasonal Migrants: Snowbirds in Canada and in Florida." Unpublished manuscript.
Martin, H. W., S. K. Hoppe, C. L. Larson, and R. L. Leon
1987 "Texas Snowbirds: Seasonal Migrants to the Rio Grande Valley." *Research on Aging* 9:134–47.
McDaniel, S. A.
1986 *Canada's Aging Population*. Toronto: Butterworths.
McInnis, M.
1971 "Age, Education and Occupation Differentials in Interregional Migration: Some Evidence for Canada." *Demography* 8:195–204.
McLeod, K. D., J. R. Parker, W. J. Serow, and N. W. Rives, Jr.
1984 "Determinants of State-to-State Flows of Elderly Migrants." *Research on Aging* 6:372–83.
McPherson, B. D.
1983 *Aging as a Social Process*. Toronto: Butterworths.
Mellor, H. W.
1962 "Retirement to the Coast." *Town Planning Review* 33:40–48.
Mercer, J.
1979 "Locational Consequences of Housing Policies for the Low-Income Elderly: A Case Study." In S. M. Golant (ed.), *Location and Environment of Elderly Population*. Toronto: John Wiley and Sons.
Messinger, H., and B. J. Powell
1987 "The Implications of Canada's Aging Society on Social Expenditures." In V. W. Marshall (ed.), *Aging in Canada: Social Perspectives*. 2nd edition. Markham: Fitzhenry and Whiteside.
Monahan, D. J., and V. L. Greene
1982 "The Impact of Seasonal Population Fluctuations on Service Delivery." *The Gerontologist* 22:160–63.
Murdock, S. H., B. Parpia, S. Hwang, and R. R. Hamm
1984 "The Relative Effects of Economic and Noneconomic Factors on Age-Specific Migration, 1960–1980." *Rural Sociology* 49:309–18.
Murphy, P. A.
1979 "Migration of the Elderly: A Review." *Town Planning Review* 50: 84–93.
Myles, J.
1982 "Social Implications of Canada's Changing Age Structure." In G. M. Gutman (ed.), *Canada's Changing Age Structure: Implications for the Future*. Burnaby: Simon Fraser University.
1984 *Old Age in the Welfare State*. Toronto: Little, Brown.
Myles, J., and M. Boyd
1983 "Population Aging and the Elderly." In D. Forcese and S. Richer (eds.), *Social Issues: Sociological Views of Canada*. Ontario: Prentice-Hall.
Nam, C. B., and S. G. Philliber
1984 *Population: A Basic Orientation*. 2nd edition. Englewood Cliffs, N.J.: Prentice-Hall.
National Council of Welfare
1982 *Financing the Canada Pension Plan*. Ottawa: Government of Canada.
1984 *Sixty-five and Older*. Ottawa: Government of Canada.

1985   *Giving and Taking: The May 1985 Budget and the Poor*. Ottawa: Government of Canada.

Neugarten, B. L.
1981   "Foreword." In E. A. Kutza, *The Benefits of Old Age*. Chicago: University of Chicago Press.

Northcott, H. C.
1984a   "The Interprovincial Migration of Canada's Elderly: 1956–61 and 1971–76." *Canadian Journal on Aging* 3:3–22.
1984b   "The Aging of Canada's Population: An Update from the 1981 Census." *Canadian Studies in Population* 11:29–46.
1985   "The Geographic Mobility of Canada's Elderly." *Canadian Studies in Population* 12:183–202.

Old Age Security Act
1984   Catalogue No. YX75-0-6-1984. Minister of Supply and Services Canada.

Pitcher, B. L., W. F. Stinner, and M. B. Toney
1985   "Patterns of Migration Propensity for Black and White American Men." *Research on Aging* 7:94–120.

Pooler, J.
1987   "Modelling Interprovincial Migration Using Entropy-Maximizing Methods." *Canadian Geographer* 31:57–64.

Population Reference Bureau
1986   *1986 World Population Data Sheet*. Washington, D.C.

Ritchey, P. N.
1976   "Explanations of Migration." In A. Inkeles (ed.), *Annual Review of Sociology* (Vol. 2). Palo Alto, California: Annual Reviews.

Rogers, T. W.
1974   "Migration of the Aged Population," *International Migration* 12:61–70.

Rowles, G. D.
1986   "The Geography of Aging and the Aged: Toward an Integrated Perspective." *Progress in Human Geography* 10:511–39.

Sant, M.
1977   "Social Disparities and Regional Policy in Britain." In A. Kuklinski (ed.), *Social Issues in Regional Policy and Regional Planning*. The Hague: Mouton.

Sell, R. R.
1983   "Analyzing Migration Decisions: The First Step — Whose Decisions?" *Demography* 20:299–311.

Serow, W. J.
1978   "Return Migration of the Elderly in the USA: 1955–1960 and 1965–1970." *Journal of Gerontology* 33:288–95.
1987   "Determinants of Interstate Migration: Differences Between Elderly and Nonelderly Movers." *Journal of Gerontology* 42:95–100.

Serow, W. J., D. A. Charity, G. M. Fournier, and D. W. Rasmussen
1986   "Cost of Living Differentials and Elderly Interstate Migration." *Research on Aging* 8:317–27.

Shaw, R. P.
1975   *Migration Fact and Theory: A Review and Bibliography of Current Literature*. Philadelphia: Regional Science Research Institute.

1985   *Intermetropolitan Migration in Canada: Changing Determinants Over Three Decades*. Catalogue No. 89–504–E. Statistics Canada. Toronto: NC Press in conjunction with Ottawa: Supply and Services Canada.

Shulman, N.
1980   "The Aging of Urban Canada." In V. W. Marshall (ed.), *Aging in Canada: Social Perspectives*. Don Mills: Fitzhenry and Whiteside.

Shulman, N., and R. E. Drass
1979   "Motives and Modes of Internal Migration: Relocation in a Canadian City." *Canadian Review of Sociology and Anthropology* 16:333–42.

Simmons, J. W.
1980   "Changing Migration Patterns in Canada: 1966–1971 to 1971–1976." *Canadian Journal of Regional Science* 3:139–62.

Statistics Canada
1982   *1981 Census Dictionary*. Catalogue No. 99–901. Ottawa: Supply and Services Canada.

Statistics Canada, Population Estimates Section, Demography Division
no date   "Summary Review of Some Strengths and Weaknesses of Elderly Migration Data Sources." Mimeo.

Stone, L. O.
1979   *Occupational Composition of Canadian Migration*. Ottawa: Statistics Canada, Minister of Supply and Services.

1978   *The Frequency of Geographic Mobility in the Population of Canada*. Ottawa: Statistics Canada, Minister of Supply and Services.

1969   *Migration in Canada: Regional Aspects*. Ottawa: Dominion Bureau of Statistics, Queen's Printer.

Stone, L. O., and C. Marceau
1977   *Canadian Population Trends and Public Policy Through the 1980s*. Montreal: McGill-Queen's University Press.

Stone, L. O., and S. Fletcher
1980   *A Profile of Canada's Older Population*. Montreal: The Institute for Research on Public Policy.

Sullivan, D. A.
1985   "The Ties that Bind: Differentials Between Seasonal and Permanent Migrants to Retirement Communities." *Research on Aging* 7:235–50.

Sullivan, D. A., and S. A. Stevens
1982   "Snowbirds: Seasonal Migrants to the Sunbelt." *Research on Aging* 4:159–77.

Trovato, F., and S. S. Halli
1983   "Ethnicity and Migration in Canada." *International Migration Review* 17:245–67.

Tucker, R. D., V. W. Marshall, C. F. Longino, and L. C. Mullins
1987   "Older Anglophone Canadians in Florida: A Descriptive Profile." Unpublished manuscript.

United Nations, Department of International Economic and Social Affairs. Statistical Office
1985   *Demographic Yearbook 1983*. New York: Publishing Division, United Nations.

United States Bureau of the Census
1984   *Current Population Reports*, Series P–23, No. 138, Demographic and

Socioeconomic Aspects of Aging in the United States. Washington, D.C.: U.S. Government Printing Office.

Vanderkamp, J.
1968   "Interregional Mobility in Canada: A Study of the Time Pattern of Migration." *Canadian Journal of Economics* 1:595–608.

Warnes, A., and C. Law
1985   "Elderly Population Distributions and Housing Prospects in Britain." *Town Planning Review* 56:292–314.

Williams, J. D., and A. J. Sofranko
1979   "Motivations for the Immigration Component of Population Turn-around in Nonmetropolitan Areas." *Demography* 16:239–55.

Winer, S., and D. Gauthier
1982   *Internal Migration and Fiscal Structure: An Econometric Study of Inter-provincial Migration in Canada.* Economic Council of Canada. Ottawa: Supply and Services Canada.

Wiseman, R. F.
1980   "Why Older People Move." *Research on Aging* 2:141–54.

Wiseman, R. F., and C. C. Roseman
1979   "A Typology of Elderly Migration Based on the Decision-Making Process." *Economic Geography* 55:324–37.

Wister, A. V.
1985   "Living Arrangement Choices Among the Elderly." *Canadian Journal on Aging* 4:127–44.

Zipf, G. K.
1946   "The P_1P_2/D Hypothesis: On the Intercity Movement of Persons." *American Sociological Review* 11:677–86.

INDEX